FROSTBIKE

FROSTBIKE

THE JOY, PAIN AND NUMBNESS
OF WINTER CYCLING

by Tom Babin

RMB

Copyright © 2014 Tom Babin, reprinted with corrections 2014

Rocky Mountain Books
www.rmbooks.com

Library and Archives Canada Cataloguing in Publication

Babin, Tom, author
    Frostbike : the joy, pain and numbness of winter cycling / Tom Babin.

Issued in print and electronic formats.
ISBN 978-1-77160-048-4 (pbk.).—ISBN 978-1-77160-050-7 (pdf).—
ISBN 978-1-77160-049-1 (html)

    1. Babin, Tom. 2. Cyclists—Alberta—Calgary—Biography. 3.
Journalists—Alberta—Calgary—Biography. 4. Cycling—Safety
measures. 5. Bicycles—Equipment and supplies. 6. Weather protection—
Equipment and supplies. I. Title.

GV1043.7.B23 2014   796.6092   C2014-904018-0
                                       C2014-904019-9

Printed in Canada

Rocky Mountain Books acknowledges the financial support for its
publishing program from the Government of Canada through the
Canada Book Fund (CBF) and the Canada Council for the Arts, and from
the province of British Columbia through the British Columbia Arts
Council and the Book Publishing Tax Credit.

Canadian   Patrimoine   Canada Council   Conseil des Arts
Heritage   canadien   for the Arts   du Canada

BRITISH COLUMBIA
ARTS COUNCIL
Supported by the Province of British Columbia

This book was produced using FSC®-certified, acid-free paper, processed
chlorine free and printed with vegetable-based inks.

For Lani

❄ ❄ ❄

CONTENTS

Season Three: The Attitude

PROLOGUE

The question emerged courtesy of a sour greeting the asphalt delivered to my hip. It was on the first corner of my commute home from work on my bicycle, a trip I had taken hundreds of times. This time, however, that corner was different. As I rounded the bend, I felt the rear end of my bike lose its grip, and my body rushed to fill the space my tire had just vacated. I slammed down on my hip first, followed by my shoulder, followed by my ego. It's not often that I crash like this, but often enough that I've recognized a series of reactions that occurs by instinct rather than reason, which explains why they are so ridiculously misprioritized:

1. First thought: "I'm never riding a bike again."
2. Pop quickly onto my feet, and then scan for bystanders to assess embarrassment level.
3. Check bike for damage.
4. Check body for damage.

This time, I went through the usual chain of reactions, but my brain took me through a fifth step.

Number five was a pair of flashbacks, or, if looked at another way, a snap assessment of a series of bad decisions that led me to my current predicament. The first bad decision was earlier that day, over the breakfast table, a bagel gripped in my teeth, as I pulled on my cycling shoes and scanned the morning newspaper's weather page. It was early November, a crisp, cold morning with a 30 per cent chance of the first snowfall of the season coming down that afternoon. Maybe I should drive my car today to avoid the snow, I thought. My bicycle was still running on smooth summer tires, and I didn't have time to install knobbier versions that would be safer on slick roads, so driving my car to work would be the smart decision. But I love riding my bike to work. It gives me energy, keeps me fit and makes me a happier, better person. So I did the math and scoffed. A 30 per cent chance of snow means there's a 70 per cent chance it won't snow. "I'm going for it," I told myself.

Bad decision number two came eight hours later, as I stared out my office window at the powdery snow slowly drifting down from the sky. That's what you get for playing the weather odds. But all was not lost. "Look at that," I told a co-worker, who kindly expressed concern about my riding a bicycle home in such weather. "It's barely accumulating. Most of the snow is melting as soon as it hits the ground. I'm going for it."

Both decisions came racing back to my mind after my post-crash assessment revealed no damage to my bike, and only surface damage to my body. I considered my options while eyeing the nearby transit stop. I could hop on the commuter train and be home, with my bike, after two bus transfers, in about 90 minutes. But my typical bike commute takes only 35. If I slowed my pace to account for the slippery conditions, especially on the corners, I could still be home before the bus. I fingered my tires: bald road slicks that had served me so well all summer long but had suddenly turned against me. Would they hold up once more this season, before being relegated to a box for the winter? Would they get me home, just once more?

It may seem like a no-brainer. Take the bus, moron. But there were other factors at play in this decision. Although I had been bicycle commuting off and on for years, I had recently started a cycling blog for the newspaper I worked at, and as such, had become, like many bike commuters, a cycling proselytizer. I had learned how a new cycling movement was making streets, and cities, better all over the world, from Minneapolis to Copenhagen to Portland to Vancouver. Cycling infrastructure, such as new traffic lanes for bicycles, was breaking the car's hold on our cities, and scaling them back toward people. Cities that encouraged cycling were seeing declines in traffic deaths, more vibrant street life, healthier citizens and reductions in pollution, especially carbon emissions. Such work gave me a new appreciation for my own bicycle commute. It had begun simply as a way of squeezing a workout into my time-crunched schedule – I could never seem to find time to hit the gym, so I figured a bicycle commute would get me to work and keep me in shape. It did that in spades, but I also found a new perspective on my city. Riding a bike opened my eyes to areas of my community I had failed to note when barrelling through in my car. Now, as I dug deeper into the personal and societal benefits of cycling, I had become an evangelist. I admonished unsuspecting friends and co-workers for wasting beautiful summer drives to work inside a car. I gushed about how bicycle commuting energized my mornings. I smugly ate massive protein-heavy lunches in front of befuddled sandwich munchers and crowed about how I was still getting leaner because of all the calories I burned commuting. I berated city planners in my blog for their failure to build adequate cycling lanes to encourage more people to commute by bike. With all that rattling around my brain, I couldn't let a little winter stop me. What would people say?

So I straddled my bike, checked that everything worked, clicked into my pedals and pushed off. I rode slowly at first, getting a feel for the slippery roads. On corners, I slowed to a crawl, the buzzing pain in my hip a constant reminder that leaning too much into a turn would mean a cruel reunion with the pavement. Thirty minutes later, I was in a groove. I kept my body upright, cornered carefully, and my confidence grew. I was slow, but making progress. As I turned into an upscale residential area on my way home, darkness had fallen, the snow muffled the sounds of the city, and something happened. I started to enjoy it. A ride that had begun as a fight against nature had turned transcendent. Traffic was light as residents huddled against the weather, and my tires cut a black path through a field of white. Light from streetlamps was reflected by the snow, creating an orange glow that gave the city an otherworldly illumination, instilling in me a strange sense of contentment, even peacefulness. My body's movement kept me warm, and even my hip was feeling better. In the darkness, I could see into the lighted windows of the homes I passed, solitary figures watching massive flat screens or huddled over computers, and I pitied them. Hiding from the weather, they had no idea of the beauty they were missing just outside their door, the kind of beauty that can only come from solitary, endorphin-induced bliss in the hushed tones of winter. That's when I crashed again.

This time I went down on the opposite side of my body, creating matching hip bruises as a kind of seasonal karmic reckoning for my winter hubris. My body went through its usual reactive process, steps one through four, but this assessment was different. This hip hurt more. My bike also took some damage; the expensive shifter I had just upgraded hung by a pathetic spring, shards of plastic on the road already being buried by snowfall. And worst of all, there were witnesses. Four teenage blondes in a massive sport utility vehicle slowly drove past with their windows rolled down. "Are you OK?" they asked. "Are you, like, hurt?" My damaged ego waved them on, even as my damaged body was screaming for a lift home.

I walked my bike the rest of the way home, which gave me lots of time to think. How could one bike ride put me in such diametrically opposed states of mind: euphoric at times, victimized at others?

Riding a bike is famously meditative – "cycling tracks will abound in Utopia," said author H.G. Wells. I had ridden home from work thousands of times, but this time, something was different. It was winter. Normally, winter brings an end to conversations about the benefits of urban cycling, especially in winter cities like mine, the prairie Canadian city of Calgary. I can't remember how many times I have heard people say spending tax dollars on bike lanes in a winter city is a waste of money because they will be impossible to use for six months of the year. Even fellow evangelists like me tend to address such arguments with a shrug and a what-are-you-gonna-do-about-it attitude toward the season. Winter is the enemy of cycling in most people's minds.

If that's the case, however, how could I have experienced such a wonderful moment on my bike in the snow, before the crash? I wanted more moments like that, without the punishing after-effect. It got me wondering. If there is a way to experience more of those blissful moments, perhaps those widely held assumptions about the impossibility of winter cycling are all wrong. Maybe riding a bike in winter can be something wonderful.

That ride home set me on a path. As I limped into the garage to park my bike, I looked up at the falling snow and made a vow that I would do what-ever I could to recapture that feeling I experienced on my ride home, no matter how brief. I set out to discover the joys that only winter cycling can bring, not only to individual riders, but also to cities and so-cieties as a whole. I wanted the answer to a big, but seldom asked, question, hopefully with as little pain as possible: despite the cold and snow, the ice and slush, the darkness and dreariness, is happy winter cycling possible? I didn't know how I would answer that question, but facing a season without riding – a months-long interval of fighting traffic, recycled air, monotony and dry lips – I knew I had to try. As soon as my hips healed.

SEASON ONE
THE BIKE

CHAPTER 1

When Edward R. Jesson, driven by a bad case of gold-rush fever, burst into the Klondike Hotel in Dawson City, Yukon, in the winter of 1900 and excitedly showed his brother-in-law the tag for his new bicycle, the reaction was swift. "What the hell are you going to do with a wheel?" his brother-in-law asked. Then, Jesson's brother-in-law gathered some of the nearby lollygaggers and old-timers, presumably to maximize the embarrassment he was about to deliver. "This brother of mine is going to try to get to Nome on a bicycle." There was laughter all around. "He's crazy."

Jesson was many things – prospector, entrepreneur, and proprietor – but he wasn't crazy. The American was still in his 20s when word spread of a gold strike near the Klondike River during the summer of 1896, prompting Jesson to blaze a path to Seattle to put together a proper prospecting outfit with dreams of striking it rich. Along with thousands of others rushing to the Yukon, Jesson headed north via the

Skagway River, after which he ended up prospecting on the Kenai Peninsula south of Anchorage, at a place optimistically named Hope and Sunrise. Like nearly all of the Yukon stampeders, however, Jesson's dream quickly soured. By 1899, he had all but given up on the mining business, instead opting to open a small store and post office in Star City, located about 200 kilometres down the Yukon River from Dawson. There were other ways to eke out a living during the gold rush.

None, however, captured the imagination like a big strike. So, in 1899, when word spread of a glittering new discovery on the western shores of Alaska, 1200 kilometres away in Nome, a new stampede began. Thousands of frustrated prospectors picked up stakes in Dawson and headed west, down the Yukon River trail, toward Alaska. Jesson couldn't resist.

Despite the region's sometimes horrendous cold spells, winter was the best time to make long trips in gold-rush Alaska. There were few roads, so traversing these areas in summer meant battling mud, insects and untamed brush. Winter, however, locked rivers into a frozen highway that offered at least the prospect of navigation. But it was rarely easy. Some parts of the river would freeze as smooth as glass making for easy transportation, encouraging at least one stubborn Norwegian, Jesson later recalled, to strap on ice skates to traverse the route, a scheme that ended when the Scandinavian broke through the ice on a big crack. More common than glass was a lurching, unpredictable obstacle course of ice, snow, rocks and earth. Rivers rarely freeze uniformly. Shallow patches and slow-moving eddies freeze first, cause backups and ice jams that create spillways that solidify unevenly. Blowing snow piles up and hardens in unpredictable ways, creating immovable boulders of ice fused with tree roots and spruce trunks. Cracks open, fill with snow, then refreeze, rendering the treacherous also invisible. For much of its distance, the Yukon River was about as similar to a skating rink as it was to Denali.

The challenge prompted feverish prospectors to try all sorts of ways of getting around Alaska and the Yukon in winter. Mules and horses were the most common, but few were hardy enough to survive the trip. So many horses were killed on the White Pass between British Columbia and Alaska on the way to the Klondike that it became known as Dead Horse Trail. One gold rusher recalled seeing at least one frozen horse carcass being used to clear snow from some parts of the Dawson-to-Nome route. The best way to get around the region was by dogsled, and in the summer of 1900, the Yukon River was teeming with mushers. Until Jesson had another idea.

❊ ❊ ❊

The Yukon gold rush coincided with another kind of fever that was settling into the imaginations of many people farther south: bicycle fever.

Only several years earlier, English inventor John Kemp Starley put together several great ideas to build the first commercially successful bicycle. The Rover, as he called it, was based on the "safety" model with two wheels of the same size on the double-triangle frame that is still used on bicycles today. It was a huge change from the famous, and dangerous, big-wheel-in-front tiny-wheel-in-back penny farthings that came the generation before. Today, we tend to think of penny farthings as an inseparable part of the Victorian era, but they never achieved mass popularity, mostly because they were expensive and terrible to ride. Crashes were so common the bikes became almost exclusively the domain of well-heeled adventure-seeking young men who didn't mind having their skulls cracked. Today, several companies build penny farthing replicas, presumably for the type of consumer who craves both Victorian-era nostalgia and attention. Despite improvements in materials, riding one still feels like a suicide attempt. Mounting them is relatively straightforward, provided you kick off with enough power to step over the seat. They can be a thrill to ride, especially when you catch a gaggle of gawkers straining their necks to watch it pass by. Dismounting it, however, is a learned art that makes you appreciate why some manufacturers in the 1800s started building mustache-shaped handlebars so riders' knees wouldn't clip them when they were inevitably ejected over the front wheel. "Headers" were just part of the ride.

The other great technological advance of the late 1800s was the development of the pneumatic tire. Before veterinarian John Boyd Dunlop perfected the idea of stretching rubber around a wheel to soften his son's bicycle ride, wheels were often made of wood or steel. Rides were so rough that penny-farthings were sometimes called "boneshakers." The pneumatic tire suddenly made bicycles comfortable. With "safety" models gaining popularity around the same time, thanks to having two wheels of the same size thereby reducing those head-crushing crashes, all that was left for a bona fide consumer craze was somebody to bring it all together.

That somebody was Starley, who incorporated the newer, safer bicycle design with the more comfortable pneumatic tires, and voilà: the bicycle became a phenomenon. Bicycle clubs quickly popped up in cities all over Europe and North America. Bike races were the most popular sporting events of the time. In New York, races in the day's biggest venues were regularly sold out, and organizers of a bicycle exhibition in 1896 at Madison Square Garden were forced to turn away as many exhibitors as they accepted for lack of space. Bicycles became symbols of feminism as women used them to get around where and when they pleased, prompting newspaper editorialists to scream about the moral decay being caused by bicycles. "Wheels," as they were often called, were seen as vehicles of the future, and were greeted with the same kind of enthusiasm for technology that greeted the iPhone 130 years later. "As for the bicycle, there is little to be said about it," wrote Charles Dickens in *All the Year Round: A Weekly Journal* in 1883. "The machine seems to have reached as near perfection as possible." A similar sentiment is captured in the scene in the film *Butch Cassidy and the Sundance Kid* when Paul Newman and Katharine Ross wheel around on a bicycle while "Raindrops Keep Falling on My Head" plays in the background, a symbol of a changing world that was leaving the old outlaws behind.

This fervour found its way to the Yukon, where Jesson plunked down a bag of prospected gold weighed out to $150 and headed over to the saloon to tell his brother-in-law about his plan to ride his new bicycle more than 1200 kilometres down the frozen Yukon River, from Dawson to Nome.

Jesson's brother-in-law can't be blamed for his skepticism. For all the fuss being made about bicycles, few people ever saw them as viable winter vehicles. Even in the enthusiastic sporting journals of the day, assumptions about bikes in the winter are the same as the ones held by most people today: you'd have to be nuts to ride in the winter. Cycling clubs spent their winters organizing racing and complaining about how horsemen and stagecoach drivers were hogging the road. Rarely, however, were they on their bikes. The idea of riding in the winter is rarely discussed, save this poem in the *London Bicycle Club Gazette* in 1878 titled "Ode to a Bicycle": "In rain or sunshine, frost or snow,/ Who goes with me where'er I go?/ And helps me seeds of health to sow? My bicycle." (The same ode goes on to thank the bicycle for saving the poet from an "angry cow.")

There is, however, little evidence that Jesson read British sporting journals while trying to eke out a living in the Yukon. That may be why he expresses in his journals an enthusiasm for the idea and the machine barely dampened by the near constant skepticism he encountered. Jesson wasn't the first stampeder to see a bicycle as a replacement for a dog team – in fact, one New York entrepreneur even marketed a "Klondike Bicycle" that was a 50-pound four-wheel job with solid rubber tires and a frame wrapped with shrunken rawhide to prevent accidental warm-skin-on-cold-metal contact – but the idea was still seen as hare-brained by most stampeders when Jesson was preparing for his ride.

When he finally acquired his bicycle, Jesson spent a week teaching himself to ride. It wasn't just staying upright that challenged him. What helped make the Yukon River traversable were the tracks in the snow and ice laid down by innumerable dogsleds that made the trip, similar in some ways to the tracks that cross-country skiers lock themselves into. Jesson had to keep his bike within those 18-inch tracks if he hoped to make progress. It wasn't easy, but he made enough progress to convince himself that getting to Nome was possible. Finally, Jesson began selling off his belongings and packing his bags. Then, as winter settled in, Jesson gave his bike a final tune-up, and pushed off onto the ice.

CHAPTER 2

I first read Jesson's journals in the middle of a cold snap only a few weeks into my first winter of bicycle commuting to work, and I was in desperate need of inspiration.

I didn't stumble into winter riding – nobody does that – but I didn't have a me-against-Mother Nature moment either. I had been commuting to work by bicycle for several summers, and had fallen in love. I was a cycling dabbler prior to that, getting wrapped up in the mountain bike craze of the 1980s during my high school years. Living close to the Rocky Mountains made it possible to hit single-track trails whenever I could convince fellow weekend warriors to join me. But life took over. A full-time job, marriage and kids made more close-to-home sports my focus. My mountain bike went into the rafters of the garage, only to be retrieved for leisurely Sunday jaunts that ended with ice cream or beer or both.

It was the traffic that convinced me to give bicycle commuting a try. I was living in Calgary, a prairie

Canadian city of a million people that has swelled in sprawling spurts over the past fifty years based on the ups and down of the price of oil. We had bought a home in an older neighbourhood, so my morning commute wasn't excessively far – less than a dozen kilometres – but traffic congestion made it unpredictable in the way commuters the world over will recognize. Some mornings, it was a smooth ten minutes. Others, jammed traffic pushed it to 45 minutes or an hour, and wore on my patience. Being stuck in traffic chips away at one's soul – at least, it gives you lots of time to think about how your soul is being chipped away – and gives you plenty of time to plot escape routes. Mine included carpooling and public transit, neither of which was satisfactory. Carpooling was tough in a small office filled with co-workers from other parts of the city, and public transit was just as unpredictable as a car, with the added bonus of urine smells and overly talkative strangers.

But sitting in a line of cars one spring day, I watched a steady stream of bicycles sail past unobstructed. Calgary, at that time, was far from a haven for bicycles. The city boasted an extensive and well-used network of paved recreational pathways, but the number of on-street bicycle lanes was exactly zero. That meant that bicycle commuters tended to be of the young and male variety: bold, confrontational and aggressive. As I sat in my bottom-of-the-line Chevrolet minivan with booster seats strapped in the back and a cassette tape deck made useless by the Napster era, I watched as cyclists weaved through lines of traffic, hopped curbs to get onto unobstructed pathways, and used the gutter lane to fly past kilometres of cars unmoving on six-lane commuter routes. Cyclists seemed to thrive in the seams of transportation infrastructure, which gave them a freedom that made me envious. That weekend, I revisited the rafters of my garage. My old mountain bike was there, rusted and wilting, but I moved past it and went for my wife's: a nice, well-used classic Raleigh mountain bike with knobby tires and upturned bar ends. It had a little rust and was painted a rather feminine shade of purple, but I was in no position to worry about fashion. I wanted to reclaim my commuting hours.

※ ❈ ※

I started gingerly, plotting out a route to work that avoided roads completely. Using a free city map from a nearby supermarket, I managed to find a route entirely on Calgary's off-road multi-use pathways, which completely dodged traffic, even though the slow, winding pathways, built for Sunday morning recreation rather than transportation, added to the distance by nearly 50 per cent. No matter. I got up early, stuffed a backpack full of work clothes, pulled on some shorts, and tentatively pushed out of the garage. That first morning was a revelation. Despite the extra distance on the path, I was shocked by how quickly I made it to work. Over the coming days, I started to notice the advantages my bicycle was offering. When collisions stalled traffic, I soared right by. When I came across construction of the kind that would have backed up traffic for hours on a road, I simply steered around it. Nothing seemed to stop me. I got faster as my legs grew stronger and I found shorter routes. As my confidence grew, I started leaving the pathways behind in some areas, entering roads and mixing it up with motor vehicles to shave off a few minutes. My initial fear of being flattened by an errant motorist never quite went away (it's still there today), but the more I did it, the more I started to understand the rhythms of the roads, and I found my place in them, however tenuous. Soon my bike commute was faster than my drive to work in my car, so it was easy to brush off occasional insults hurled by motorists who erroneously felt they should have exclusive use of the road.

Over the coming weeks, I also noticed some

changes in myself. I started to feel stronger from the exercise, and had more energy through the day. My body was consuming more resources, so I ate more, even as I grew leaner, which annoyed my calorie-watching colleagues who eyed my massive lunches with envy. At the end of the day, rather than fitful nighttime sleeping, I felt my body craving rest, and I quickly fell into deep slumbers. I wanted to ride my bike to work every day. I was hooked.

This lasted through the summer and into the fall. As the days grew colder, I dressed for them, and encountered few problems. But when that first snowfall hit, I did what most people do with their bicycles. I unhooked the brakes, deflated the tires, and put it back into the rafters of my garage. Riding a bike is something you do in the summer, right?

But a funny thing happened that winter. Almost immediately, I started to feel tired and grumpy at work. Lethargy set in, which went beyond the usual Vitamin D-starved winter doldrums so many of us get. It didn't take me long to realize what my body was missing – what my mind was missing – was that daily bike ride. One of the nice things about riding my bike to work was that it did two things at once, commuting and exercising. As the dad of two busy elementary school-aged children, I found it nearly impossible to squeeze workouts into my schedule, so bike commuting was an easy solution. Without it, my workouts ebbed, and my body with it. Perhaps even worse, driving to work put me back in commuter perdition, stuck in my crappy minivan listening to grunge-era cassette tapes and loathing every minute of it.

As soon as the snow melted off the streets that spring, I was back on my bike, and thinking about how I could overcome the next winter. On a bike, you aren't bombarded by the sights and sounds of our digital age, so it gives you time to think – another thing I missed during my winter in vehicular exile – so I spent the summer pondering something that turned out to be a big question. It seemed to be a simple inquiry, but when I first started thinking about it, I had no idea how involved it really was. Eventually, my search for its answer took me around the world, and changed the way I look at transportation, our cities, our attitudes, and, most importantly, myself.

Is it possible to happily ride a bike in winter?

CHAPTER 3

On foggy winter morning in Vienna in the mid-2000s, during which the thermometer reached −20°c, Michael Embacher checked over one of the strangest bicycles he had ever owned, which is saying something considering he has perhaps the world's greatest collection of rare, unique and downright bizarre bikes. He was standing on the edge of a frozen lake, one of many that dot the Austrian capital region, below trees turned to icicles by hoar frost. He went through the checklist. Frame? It was secure, despite being more than 40 years old. Back tire? His last attempt at riding this bike failed because of a puncture, so he gave it a squeeze. It was solid, despite the dozens of spikes that protruded from it menacingly. Front blade? In place of the front wheel was an ice skate blade had been fixed to metal rods connected to the front forks. The rods were intact, the blade sharp. He was ready to go.

Gingerly, he stepped onto the ice, and mounted the bike. It had a single fixed-gear transmission, which meant that, unlike the freewheels installed on most bikes, he wouldn't be able to stop pedalling. The drivetrain was threaded directly onto the rear hub so his pedals moved in co-ordination with the back wheel, forwards or backwards. This type of transmission is standard on track racing bikes, and has been increasingly adopted by urbanites, especially bicycle couriers, who say it gives them more control and durability, because of its simplicity. It also, however, meant that Embacher's bike had no brakes. Fixies, as they've come to be called, can be stopped by putting reverse pressure on the drivetrain. But it takes practice. And Embacher had never tried it on ice. And never with a back wheel riddled with medieval-looking spikes that threatened to brain him if he took a tumble.

I first spotted the Capo Elite "Eis," as Embacher, calls it, years later when the bicycle appeared in the pages of Embacher's book *Cyclepedia: A Century of Iconic Bicycle Design*, a lovingly designed coffee-table tome featuring photographs of his collection. The bizarre hybrid jumped out at me, so I managed to track Embacher down in Vienna and left him a telephone message. He returned my call within minutes and, in his German accent, enthusiastically recounted the story of his bizarre ice bike.

For years, Embacher had lusted over the bike after he had seen it around his home city in the hands of its creator, an 88-year-old bicycle fanatic who was a member of the city's small but passionate cadre of collectors. Embacher was perhaps the most prominent member of this group, with a massive collection that includes such odd jobs as a military-issued folding bike designed for paratroopers, and a pink Swedish bike made of plastic that was shipped to customers in pieces like an Ikea bookshelf. The owner of the "Eis" had built the ice bike originally by modifying a pair of 1966 frames from Capo, a small but well-regarded Austrian bicycle maker formed in the 1930s by two former pro bike racing brothers. Likely inspired by photos from the 1930s when an ice bike craze took over Vienna, the owner removed the front tires from his Capos and affixed a kind of skate blade on a tripod, thus building one unique ice bike for himself and one for his wife. By the time Embacher spotted the machine, the wife's had fallen into disrepair, but the designer was still taking his out during Austrian winters, so he refused to sell it. "It was in his collection, but he used it every day," Embacher told me. "He was emotional about the bike. He didn't want to sell it." Embacher cooled his heels, but when his first book came out, things changed. Seeing the care that Embacher took with his collection of old bikes, the old man caved. Embacher had his bike.

Embacher makes a point of ensuring all the bikes in his collection are roadworthy, so on a winter morning bleached by fog, he found himself on the shores of a frozen Austrian lake nervously straddling his newly acquired Capo Elite "Eis." Off he pushed, and into the mist he pedalled. Embacher says he was surprised by the speed of the bike, and its handling. The spiked tire propelled him swiftly, and he found the skate blade offered great control. Provided he didn't lean into his turns too much, he had no problem with the bicycle's manoeuvrability. He bombed around on the ice with a smile on his face, even if he couldn't see because of the fog. But that lack of visibility brought some new meaning to the ride, which Embacher recalled to me with gusto. "It was really a fantastic ride," he said. "It was really an amazing day. With the fog, I couldn't see the horizon line, so it's like I was riding into nothing." Then he laughed. "It was like a rebirth." Embacher's wasn't the first bicycle built for snow and ice. Almost as soon as the first bicycles started gaining popularity, ingenious entrepreneurs were modifying them for use in winter. There are dozens of U.S. patents dating to the late 1800s for ice and snow bikes. In

April of 1892, for example, John Stevens, an inventor living in Hartford, Connecticut, who later went on to create several contraptions to help lower caskets into graves, submitted a patent application for an "Ice Velocipede." In its quaint Victorian style, the schematic drawings included with the patent make it look like the great-great-great-grandfather of the Capo Elite "Eis," complete with a miniature ski in place of the front wheel and deadly looking spikes out back. "(To be) used on surfaces covered by snow or ice, and is also constructed as to be readily changed so as to be used on ordinary roads like other vehicles of its class," the patent optimistically reads. Other inventions from the time include those that look more like tricycles, with two skis at the back flanking a front tire that more closely resembles the blade of a circular saw. Hussong's "Ice Velocipede" from 1885 lacked pedals; the user operated two hand cranks back and forth to move the machine across the ice, which I imagine would build users' bodies into something completely opposite of those you see on professional cyclists today, with spindly superfluous legs dangling below longshoreman's arms, rather than the reverse.

Researching these ancient models was the first step in my winter cycling journey, because to answer my big question, I quickly realized I need to pose a second, smaller question, one that arose every time I mounted my wife's purple mountain bike and warily eyed the snow in front of me: what's the perfect winter bike?

In the time I had been bicycle commuting, I had adopted a mantra I came to know as "learn as you go," or, perhaps more accurately, "learn as you screw up." I decided to apply that mantra to my pursuit of my big question about winter cycling, so as the temperature dropped and the days shortened, I decided to learn as I went. Within a few days, I had an easy answer to my initial question. The reason you don't see many bikes with ice skates for front tires is because you don't need them. In fact, I found that I didn't need anything special for winter cycling. For the first few weeks of winter, the snowfall was light and it melted quickly, so the roads and pathways stayed clear, and my ride was a smooth as it had been in the summer. As the weather grew colder, I traded in my shorts and T-shirt for some narrow-legged pants and a hoodie, and life was good. Winter cycling, it seemed, looked an awful lot like summer cycling. It was fun and easy and fast. Then the snowstorm hit.

By this time, I had taken a new job that was farther from home, so my commute had climbed to about 16 kilometres each way, which, on a good summer day, took me about 35 minutes. The hardest part was the river valley that lay between home and work, which meant I encountered hills on both ends. In the summer, I came to view the hills as a challenge – I actually enjoyed the heart-pounding climb that came at the end of all my rides. But when the snowstorm hit, the hills took on a new and menacingly slippery personality.

That morning, the snow raced out of the sky as if in a hurry to accumulate, but I managed to fight through it on roads until I reached the top of a pathway that angled down a hill into the Elbow River valley and, eventually, toward my destination. I stopped my bike and eased towards the crest of the hill to gauge the condition of the paved pathway that snaked downward. The snow had already proven slick. I had wobbled my way this far by trying to stay within the tire tracks of cars that had come before, but drifting out of those narrow confines forced me into a panicked handlebar shake as my heart leapt into my throat. It was unbecoming, and dangerous. Those near-crashes made me wary of the speed I would pick up going down the hill. When I looked down, however, I was surprised that I didn't see a pathway blanketed with shimmering wet sleet, rather a distinct trail pockmarked with footprints and streaked with the tracks of cyclists who came before me. It played with my ego. Perhaps I was being dramatic. If other people had already braved this hill, why couldn't I?

I pushed off, squeezing the brakes hard, and started down the slope. At first, it was smooth going. But as the slope steepened, I struggled to keep my speed down. I clutched too hard on the brakes and locked the wheels, putting me into a full skid. Before I knew what was happening, gravity was pulling me down at its own pace, no matter how much I gnashed. I was losing control, so I put my feet down, something any mountain biker will tell you is a bad idea, which hastened my fall. In the next moment, I was removing myself from a snow-caked bush after a slow-motion crash that would have been hilarious had I seen it on YouTube and it involved somebody else. Sheepishly, I walked the rest of the way down, only to slip off my feet as I neared the bottom of the hill. Sitting on my ass as blowing snow enveloped me, that question I thought I had quickly answered came back to me. I may not need Embacher's ice bike, with its spikes and skate blade, but perhaps there is something to the idea of finding the perfect winter bicycle.

CHAPTER 4

Early in my career as a reporter, I worked for a small-town newspaper in Alberta. On weekends, life in small-town Alberta isn't exactly bustling for an aspiring newspaper reporter. Nothing happens, especially in the winter when the whole town is at the hockey rink. To combat that, and ensure the pages of the newspaper got filled, I got in the habit of wandering. On slow weekends, I'd seek out new locations in the pursuit of stories, which usually ended with earnest write-ups about craft fairs or the personality of a new bull at the nearby bison farm. On one particularly quiet day, I passed by a small frozen lake and noticed a shack on the middle of the ice. It was a cold day, so I pulled my car over, grabbed my camera and set out toward the shack, intending to tell the story of a lonely ice fisherman so committed to his hobby that he had braved the coldest that winter could offer. But when I stepped out of my car, I heard a buzzing that drew my attention. I walked toward the sound, around a bend in the lake, and came upon dozens of vehicles and what seemed like hundreds of people gathered on the ice around a path in the middle of the lake that had been cleared of snow. Tearing around the ice were dozens of motorcycles. I had stumbled upon the little-known world of ice racing, in which motorcycle riders on studded tires race around the ice while friends and family members drink beer stored in snowbanks. Three hours later, with a camera and a pen frozen into uselessness (note to aspiring northern reporters: use a pencil), I had my weekend story.

On one particularly slippery commuting moment years later, the image of those motorcycles and their studded tires inexplicably popped into my head. Despite my initial crash on the hill, I managed to make it to work that day, and thanks to a few days of driving, some favourable weather and some city snow plowing, I managed to resume my commutes shortly thereafter, with little drama. But I was still worried about the next snowfall. My experience on the hill taught me to pay attention to weather conditions, and when the snow did come again I needed to be prepared.

I had quickly given up on the idea of replacing my front tire with a skate blade because I wasn't riding on a frozen lake. I needed the traction of a tire because my rides consisted mostly of plowed pavement dotted with patches of snow and ice. As those slippery patches began to appear with more frequency, I remained wary, but found ways around them. Mostly, I simply avoided them or dismounted and walked. If I was forced onto ice, I found riding directly over it worked, provided I didn't turn, lean, brake or descend a slope. Packed snow, I quickly learned, was little problem. The knobs on my mountain bike tires could find good traction. Loosely packed slush, however, was dangerous. Not because it was especially slippery, but because it seemed to lift and carry my bike in unpredictable ways, and because it was usually found in the gutter lane of a road that was filled with motorists who expressed their displeasure with sharing the road by passing as closely as possible while I wobbled over the slush. Worst of all was something called snirt, a mixture of snow and dirt pounded into the consistency of mashed potatoes that offered no traction and even less certainty. So even after a few weeks of winter riding, I still lacked confidence on the slippery bits.

During one of those crossroads crash moments – a millisecond between the times you feel your back tire slide out from under you and you either hit the pavement or shakily recover, the image of those ice motorcycles popped into my head. If their two wheels could find traction on ice, why couldn't I?

The key, I soon learned was to use studded tires. After the fact, it seemed like a bit of a no-brainer, but I hadn't thought of studded bicycle tires before because I didn't feel I needed them. But that changed. Winter is different everywhere, and Calgary's winter character is ice. The region is stricken (or blessed, depending on your perspective) with a unique weather phenomenon called chinooks, a warm, dry *föhn* wind that blows over the Rocky Mountains periodically through the winter, and offers a welcome respite from the cold. Not only do chinooks bring in dizzyingly quick temperature changes – in 1962, a chinook brought the temperature up in southern Alberta to 22°C (71°F) from −19°C (−28°F) in one hour; that's a 41-degree C (99°F) change – but they also melt snow quickly. When the warm winds die down, however, that ice water refreezes and we're left with roads and pathways snaked with channels of newly formed ice. These were the moments when studded tires seemed like a good idea.

There's nothing revolutionary about studded tires. Winter riders have been using them for generations. There are all sorts of studded bicycle tires available in bike shops these days, in a range of prices, but because I was still riding a decade-old girly purple mountain bike that was slowly breaking down from the rigours of commuting, it seemed silly to spend good money on new tires. So, after I asked around a bit, and did a little Internet research, I convinced myself that I could build my own.

Off to the hardware store I went. I emerged with a $9 box of flat-headed screws and, naturally, a roll of duct tape. I dug out an old pair of knobby tires from the garage and, for the next few hours, aided by my skeptical eight-year-old son, I drilled dozens of small holes through the tire. Then, I sank the screws through the holes so the sharp ends protruded. I finished by coating the inside of the tire with duct tape so that the blunt ends of the screws wouldn't puncture the tire tube. Voilà: DIY studded tires. They weren't perfect. Some of the screws protruded a little too far, and more than once I snagged my jacket (the money I saved by DIYing the tires ended up being spent on a new jacket; there's a lesson here), but, happily, the spikes made some plain old mountain bike tires look a little bad ass. I felt like Mad Max in a toque. But I still didn't know if they'd work. I needed to test them. The tires rolled fine on asphalt, provided I didn't lean too much into the turns because that would bring the studs into contact with the road and the vibration would make my jaw bounce. What I really needed was some ice to test them. So one Sunday morning, I awoke early and headed to the lake where the idea first entered my mind. If these homemade studs can work on a frozen lake, I reasoned, they would work anywhere.

There hadn't been snowfall in a while, so the lake was clear and clean, and judging by the pickup trucks parked next to ice-fishing shacks, it was thick enough to hold my weight. Yet, I was a bit nervous. There must be an ancient part of the human brain that instinctively prevents us from taking bicycles on ice, because I couldn't seem to bring myself to take the leap. I did a few laps of the parking lot and tested out my studs on some packed snow. With the studs arranged off centre, rolling upright and straight made for a smooth ride. The screws only engaged with the ground when I leaned into a turn. I ambled into a few corners on some packed snow to get a feel for the studs, and I was surprised by how much security they offered. At least, they made me feel secure; I still wasn't sure the feeling was real. I still imagined myself kissing asphalt prior to every turn. My confidence rose with every corner, and I realized that, until now, I had been significantly adjusting my riding on slippery roads. In the summer, it's natural to lean deeply into turns, but I had subconsciously stopped doing that in the winter. My turns on snow and ice were slow, gradual, upright and, I realized, a little wussy. For a passerby, it must have been like watching a senior citizen steer a bumper car. The more I rode on my studs, however, the closer I got to the world of reasonable turning.

Finally, I decided it was time. I walked onto the ice of the lake, took a deep breath, and pushed off. Going in a straight line was no problem. My back tire slipped a little when I pushed the pedals too much, but it was mostly smooth going. I couldn't, however, ride straight forever. The shoreline approached, so I had to turn. I spread my legs to stop any sudden falls, leaned gingerly into a turn and, to my surprise, the studs grabbed hold of the ice and kept my bike underneath me. Success. Modest success, but success nonetheless.

I circled around the lake a few times, my confidence growing until I pushed things a little too hard and frightened myself with a slip. My homemade tires weren't perfect – I hadn't placed the studs exactly right, so not every turn was as smooth as I would have liked – but I figured that a store-bought pair of studded tires would solve that problem, if I ever decided to spend the money on a pair.

More importantly, I felt like I had cracked some kind of secret winter cycling code. There was a solution to the problem of ice. In fact, it was the first real challenge of winter that I had overcome, and it felt good. For the first time, I felt like I had some control over the winter. I had already extended my riding season by more than a month, and now I felt like I could ride indefinitely.

The studded tires I built remained on my bike, and as the snow and ice solidified for the season, I turned into a convert. I started recommending them to anybody who asked, and a few who didn't. Eventually, my DIY tire screws started drifting and tearing away and, in the midst of a warm spell, I removed the shredded rubber, and I never felt the need to replace the studs. They had done their job by giving me the confidence I needed to figure out how to better ride on winter roads. Without them, I encountered the occasional slip that sent my stomach lurching, but I was becoming a better winter rider, and was better able to recognize the danger zones of loose slush and black ice. I also adjusted my route to work, in an almost subconscious way, in an attempt to find the sweet spot between roads that were too busy, and roads that weren't busy enough for a snowplow to clear, and my knobby mountain bike tires carried me through the season with few problems.

For weeks, I rode in a zone of winter cycling bliss. I felt like I had found my place. The joys of cycling were coming back to me. I felt strong and healthy, and I started to embrace cycling in a way that was slightly different than in summer. I started to realize that riding a bike in winter isn't just different than other kinds of cycling; it's different than everything else. Two tires cutting through the snow blends fulfillment and recklessness into a unique feeling of empowerment. Sure, riding in poor weather is something every cyclist does eventually, but besting the rain or the early morning chill is more accident than accomplishment. Besting winter on a bike, however, is an act of defiance. It's a challenge to one of the few remaining intrusions of nature into modern life. I often think about literature in which winter is a metaphor for death. Poet Thomas Hardy was hardly subtle when he wrote "Winter's dregs made desolate" in "The Darkling Thrush." Later, he called the wind to a "death's lament." Yet, cycling through such apparent desolation made me feel so good that I started to think Hardy was a drama queen. I was beating down our harshest weather with little more than my wits and some steel. That feeling is what gives a good winter ride its transcendence. A nice ride in the summer is something to brag about to your friends. A good ride in the winter is something you quietly put adjacent to your heart; an unspoken victory filed away for times of weakness and need, to be pulled out when you require a reminder of what you are capable of. And I was doing it all on an aging, purple girls' mountain bike.

Then, one day, that all changed. I saw it: a machine that forced me to rethink everything I had learned about the perfect winter bike.

CHAPTER 5

In the 1990s, a group of jocks, idealists and moderately masochistic athletes with something to prove, mostly to themselves, would gather in the middle of winter in snow-covered fields around Alaska. Inspired by the epic Iditarod sled dog race that cuts through the snow from Anchorage to Nome, this group would set out on long – I mean long – off-road bike races through the snow. These races were sometimes 500 kilometres, sometimes up to 1600 kilometres in the case of Iditarod Trail Invitational, a.k.a. the Iditasport. Part of the group was a motley crew of mountain bike enthusiasts and dedicated tinkerers who were always looking for an edge by modifying their bikes to better traverse snow and ice.

One year, a bike enthusiast named Steve Baker appeared with a bike design that nobody had seen before. Baker, who had been tinkering with winter bike ideas for more than 15 years under the company name Icicle Bicycles, building everything from sturdy road bikes to models with elevated chain stays, had been crafting wider tires for some time. But this year, he had managed to weld together three rims and affix them to a bike frame with unusually large forks. The result was a kind of Frankenbike, a mutant mountain bike with massively wide tires.

Most people did little more than chuckle at the creation, but when the bike seemed to get past patches of snow and ice that trapped traditional mountain bikes, fellow Alaskan Mark Gronewald took note. Gronewald saw how the wide tires seemed to enable the bike to float over the snow, while bikes with skinnier tires tended to break through and become lodged. On ice and rocks, the wide tires also seemed to have more stability and the ability to roll over larger obstacles. Gronewald, also a tinkerer, went home to think. He did little more than that until 1999, when Gronewald and his friend, fellow winter bike enthusiast John Evingson, visited the Interbike Trade Show in Las Vegas. The annual event is the industry's biggest showcase, and draws all the big industry names alongside small-scale builders and retailers like Gronewald and Evingson, who built and sold bikes through their company Wildfire Designs in Palmer, Alaska.

While browsing the booths and catching up on industry trends, the pair came across a man named

Ray Molina, a Texan who made a living guiding mountain bikers into Mexico. Molina's problem was that traditional mountain bikes got mired in the Mexican sand, sinking deep into the loose areas and refusing to budge until the rider got off and pushed. Molina figured wider tires would fix the problem, so he designed wheels with three-and-a-half inch tires that required low pressure in order to seemingly float over the sand. He had set up a facility in Mexico to produce them. What he hadn't quite figured out, however, was how to build the perfect bike frame that could accommodate the tires.

When they saw Molina's wheels, Gronewald and Evingson had one of those eureka moments. They both imagined those massive tires cruising over the Alaskan snow. They arranged for delivery of a few of Molina's tires, and when they returned north, they got to work, Gronewald designing around those huge wheels, and Evingson, an iron and pipeline worker, welding frames. Drawing up full-scale drafts on paper, Gronewald came up with a few important innovations to accommodate those massive wheels. The tires, for example, were too wide for traditional hubs. Rather than design a custom-built ultra-wide hub, Gronewald was determined to design a bike that used commonly available parts so they could be easily fixed if something went wrong. To accommodate those thick tires, he managed to incorporate a traditional hub that was off-centred but still enabled the wheel to rotate around it. They started calling their designs fat bikes, based on the girth of the tires.

Gronewald was soon spotted riding around Alaska on his new designs. At first, people would laugh at him. It's easy to see why. Fat bikes, on first blush, look like they were designed by a cartoonist. The tires seem absurdly wide, like a mountain-bike monster truck. But by February 2000, Evingson and Gronewald had built four fat bikes for use in that year's Iditasport, for themselves and a couple of friends, at a cost of about $5,000 each (a set of tires alone ran more than $1,000). "People were sort or snickering at us when they first saw the bikes," Gronewald later told me, with a laugh. "The bigger tires make a huge difference, and people started to see that. (Other riders) would see the bigger tracks and try to ride in them, and they still couldn't make it. We were just armchair riders and we were leaving some of those pros in the dust."

Soon, fat bikes started being ridden to victory in the biggest of those Alaskan races, and people started taking them seriously. Racers and recreationalists were coming to Gronewald and Evingson with money to spend. Their company became the first to commercially offer fat bikes for sale. They were, however, far from a runaway success. The market, even in Alaska, for expensive winter bikes was just too small. In 2000, they told the local newspaper their dream was to sell 25.

In the meantime, however, modifications kept coming. Gronewald and Evingson and other Alaskans improved on the hubs and spokes, and offered recessed cross tubes to protect their precious bits when dismounting the bikes in deep snow. Better tires meant the air pressure could be toyed with, offering soft rides that negated the need for expensive suspension systems, and more pressure when the ground was harder. Fat bikes, however, remained on the fringes. It was tough to envision huge consumer demand for a machine that carried on the tradition of seemingly delusional Alaskans cycling through the wilderness in the middle of winter. "They were a hard sell. I could just see the suspicion on people's faces when I talked about them," Gronewald says. "Every one I sold was a hard sell."

Others, however, had similar visions. Down in California around the same time, Dan Hanebrink, a former NASA engineer, was growing frustrated with his attempts at building the ultimate off-road bike. It was the early 1990s, and the veteran mountain biker was living in Big Bear Lake, California, where he could scratch his cycling itch all summer long. Come wintertime, however, his bike became useless. He still wanted to ride, but his derailleurs gummed up with wet clay, and snow packed into his tires, robbing them of traction. His attempts at winter off-road biking usually ended with him walking, wet and shivering, back to his car for the drive home. "I wouldn't accept that," he told me.

Unlike most frustrated winter cyclists, however, Hanebrink could do something about it. Soon, he was mulling ideas about building a better winter bicycle. He put his aerospace-engineer-trained brain to work – he had long worked around cars and motorcycles, in addition to his work with NASA – and before long, he had a mental image of that winter ride. Most bike engineers count their victories by shaving a few ounces off the weight of a frame. Hanebrink focused on a part of the bike that also drew the attention of those winter trail riders up in Alaska: the tires. What Hanebrink had in mind was a bicycle that operated on a different principle than most off-road bikes of the time, which used knobs on the tires to grab the earth and propel riders forward. Hanebrink envisioned fat tires, fatter even

than the mountain bike tires that had come to dom-
inate the North American bicycle market through
the 1980s and '90s, and fatter even than those that
were being tinkered with in Alaska. He was thinking about tires from a motorcycle or quad. Eventually,
he settled on golf cart tires, wider and with a smaller
diameter than traditional bike tires, inflated to balloon levels that wouldn't grip the snow so much as
cruise over it. He soon developed a frame that could
accommodate such tires, but his prototype had the
same problem as the mountain bikes that drove his
frustration in the first place. The bike seemed to float
over the snow just like he had envisioned, but the
knobby tires made it difficult to pedal. He tried several different types of tires, but none seemed to propel the bike forward in the way he wanted. Then, he
had an idea.

Hanebrink loaded his bike into the back of
his truck, and drove out of the snow toward the
coast. He was headed for the beach. Anybody
who has ever been stymied in an attempt to take
a pleasant bike ride down the beach knows what
Hanebrink was after: loosely packed sand acts
much the same as loosely packed snow. It can be
hell to pedal through. Tires sink into the sand and
stick – end of ride. That's exactly what Hanebrink

found. The bike wouldn't move forward in the way he wanted. But when he dismounted and looked back, the sand sent a message that he never received in the snow. He got down on his hands and knees and looked back at the marks the tires left in the sand. There were large square holes left by the knobs of the tires sunk deep into the beach. The tires may have been floating on the sand like he wanted, but the treads of the tires were getting mired. Pushing the bike with enough force to dislodge those treads from the sand was using a huge amount of energy. Immediately, he drove to a friend's house and, using a bread knife, cut the knobs off the tires. Back later at the beach, Hanebrink had his own eureka moment. "It was a huge breakthrough," he says.

More than 20 years later, I came across the Hanebrink X-Bike, or Extreme Terrain bike, in a television news clip from Antarctica. Helen Skelton, the tough and tiny host of BBC Kids science show *Blue Peter*, had become the first person in the world to ride a bike to the South Pole. Her vehicle of choice was a custom-designed Hanebrink, built without any plastic, which would crack in the cold. It had a leather seat, and brakes were installed only on the back wheel to reduce weight. Images of her riding over the pole on those eight-inch wide tires were beamed around the world. For anyone who ever heard the stories from the golden age of Antarctic exploration, of Amundsen and Scott's deadly race across the ice, and Shackleton's harrowing plight to stay alive, the image of this cute-as-a-button adventurer, with her TV-host smile beaming from beneath her fur-lined hood, her mittens looking two sizes too big, was an arresting one. I, however, couldn't take my eyes off her bike.

After I heard Skelton's story, I got in touch with Hanebrink to hear the story of how his bike made it to the pole. Hanebrink seemed gratified with Skelton's South Pole adventure, but seemed to view it as a bit of a sideshow. In his mind, the bike's usefulness in extreme conditions had already been proven several years earlier when polar explorer Doug Stoup, the first American to ski to the South Pole, used Hanebrink's X-Bike to bomb around Antarctica, racking up more than 300 kilometres on the odometer before a huge Antarctic storm grounded him. The experience earned the bike a spot in *Time* magazine's "Best Inventions of 2003." Stoup was never able to come up with financing for a cycling assault on the pole, though, which opened the door for Skelton.

By then, however, Hanebrink had moved on to bigger ideas (he told me with some satisfaction that he forced the BBC to pay for Skelton's bike, despite their hints that offering it free of charge would be good publicity for him). Hanebrink was after a mass market. He had moved on to creating an electric version of the X-Bike, which he was focused on selling for about $7,600 US, compared to the $6,000 price for his pedal-powered model.

That mass market, however, was proving tougher to conquer than the South Pole. Up in Alaska, mainstream success also eluded Gronewald, even when he started outsourcing frame building to keep his costs down. With a limited market in Alaska, he could never seem to get over the hump.

Then, in 2004, Gronewald received a prototype fat tire and a request to test it out. The tire came from a representatives of Minnesota bicycle company Surly. Surly initially gained popularity by being on the front lines of industry trends through the 2000s and 2010s. They found a niche by being at the right place at the right time, by offering well-made fixed-gear bicycles to young, hip urban riders who had started building their own after being inspired by downtown bike couriers. Gronewald was flattered the company had noticed his design, and knew the company was working on some kind of model with wider wheels, but didn't think much of it. He was still struggling to sell every bike he built, so he couldn't imagine a big company pouring much money into the designs.

Then, in 2005, Surly's catalogue featured a new design called a Pugsley that looked completely bizarre to most people, except, perhaps, for a few people in Alaska, including Gronewald. The Pugsley looked like a traditional mountain bike, but had four-inch-wide tires, a two- or sometimes three-fold increase in size over traditional mountain bikes. It was a bona fide fat bike, similar to the ones Gronewald had been selling for years. It was the first time a major manufacturer had mass-produced a fat bike, earning the company reactions that were not unlike those Gronewald first noted: curiosity and skepticism. Gronewald says he was surprised how similar the Pugsley was to his design, right down to the off-centred hub.

Within five years, however, fat-biking had grown into one of the fastest growing sectors of the North American bicycle market, worth tens of millions of dollars. By 2012, fat bikes had become so popular that Surly could barely keep up with demand. Today, several companies market different fat bikes, and the Pugsley is seen as a pioneering model, one of those bikes bound to go down in industry lore as a groundbreaker, like the Specialized Stumpjumper or Schwinn Black Phantom.

Hanebrink is still pushing his designs, and grumbles a bit that he deserves a bigger chunk of the winter-bike industry. Gronewald, however, has given up trying to sell fat bikes, and has got accustomed to people telling him he was ripped off. He's a little more philosophical about it, saying there's no way he could have pushed the bikes into the mainstream the way a big industry player like Surly has. "It's just the way business goes," he says, a little ruefully. "The early innovators, they have the mind to innovate but not for business." These days, when Gronewald hits the trails of Alaska and sees fat bikes everywhere, cruising through the snow alongside cross-country skiers, he doesn't feel bitter, except, perhaps, when people see his designs and accuse him of knocking off Surly's. He's happy he had a hand in popularizing the sport. "I had no idea it would get this huge," he says. "I think it's a good thing as an alternative to driving and getting people out and active in winter. I could be bitter, but life is too short."

There's a group of purists who feel the Alaskans deserve the credit for inventing the fat bike (likewise, Hanebrink feels he deserves a little love), but that's not completely fair. Surly may have built on the designs of the Alaskans, but without the company's marketing muscle, and the ability to offer lower prices thanks to overseas manufacturing, fat-biking would still likely be a fringe hobby for a group of quirky Alaskans. Surly's success has made things tough for both Gronewald and Hanebrink, but it's hard to imagine how fat-biking could have progressed so far without Surly. Gronewald and Hanebrink may simply be the latest victims of American capitalism.

By the time I had begun dabbling in winter riding, fat bikes had become a kind of you-gotta-try-this cult hit. Only weeks into winter and all of the bike shops in my city had sold out. "We can't even get them from the manufacturer," one bike-store owner had told me. Thankfully, the store still had a few demo models for customers to try out. So one Friday morning in December, after I had convinced the only other person I knew with the day off to join me (my 60-year-old father, who is also one of the hardiest cyclists I know), I loaded a couple fat-bike demos on a rack on the back of my minivan, and we went in search of some snow-covered trails.

We ended up in Fish Creek Provincial Park, a kind of jackpine Central Park for Calgarians that had originally been a getaway on the fringes of the city, but had become an urbanite playground as the city sprawled around it. The park's mountain bike trails weren't exactly Olympic calibre, but there was a fresh snowfall on the ground, and for a couple of fat bike rookies, we figured that would be enough.

As we pulled on our tuques, we chuckled at the absurdity of the machines. We had borrowed a pair of Salsa Mukluks, a competitor to the Pugsley's early designs, and with massive tires built by Surly, they looked rather ridiculous, like a caricature of a mountain bike drawn by a six-year-old. They lacked suspension, and as soon as I mounted it I knew why. As we pedalled over the parking lot toward the trails, the tire pressure was so low that I gently bounced along as if riding a rocking horse. We passed a mom piling her kids onto a sled and she stared with a bemused look on her face. I blushed. What had we got ourselves into?

We rode up into the packed snow of the trail trepidatiously at first, testing out the snowy tarmac. The bikes rolled along smoothly. Traction, which is sometimes impossible to come by in winter, was easy to find. Riding the trail felt no different than the summer. We were giddy at the prospect of riding a bike over snow that wouldn't dump us at every opportunity, but at the same time we were in a bit of disbelief. Both of us had spent our lives negotiating snow and ice and we had developed a sense of its limits, so we didn't quite trust the security we felt on the low-pressure tires. So I started putting them to the test. I rode up the shoulders of the trail, and went hard at the dips and rises, searching for the boundaries. Try as I might, I couldn't slip. The bike seemed tailor-made for loose-packed snow. The riding was slow – the huge tires and low gearing had us spinning furiously to generate little velocity – but we were so taken with our stability we hardly noticed.

After we had a few kilometres behind us, we came across a pair of cross-country ski tracks laid in the snow, an informal set venturing into the trees. In the summer, this was a single-track trail made for mountain bikes, but in the winter, covered with snow, it was mostly ignored. In fact, if this skier had never broken the trail, we would have missed it. We shared a quick glance and we were gone, veering off the safe trail that had been packed by the legions of hikers who had come before us, and into the good stuff. Loose virgin powder, not exactly a skiers' dream – the snow was only as deep as our calves – but a good test for our fat bikes. We geared down and plowed into it, our massive tires churning out dry snow behind us. For more than an hour we took these trails, some of them laden with cross-country ski tracks but most forgotten for the winter. We went up hills and down, negotiated downed logs that were covered by snow, climbed over rocks and through frozen gullies. We were hung up only occasionally. One steep hill was too much for us and as the slope increased, the snow proved too loose and slippery. A couple of times, we hit pockets that brought us to a standstill – the bikes sank too deeply into piles of snow the consistency of icing sugar, and we simply couldn't push through them. What we did find, however, was the joy of discovering something new. Trails that we had closed off from our minds when the first snow fell were now accessible. It opened up a whole new way of thinking about cycling and about winter. It was fun.

One other thing happened before we pulled back into the parking lot at the end of the day. At one point, as we followed some ski tracks through the trees, we were suddenly dumped into a clearing. Before we knew where we were, we found ourselves in the middle of a frozen creek, the ski tracks moving off downstream. We stopped, worried about the strength of the ice, and worried about breaking the rules of parks that require cyclists to stay on designated paths. But I couldn't resist dawdling on the ice a bit. I took a couple of big loops before making my way back to the trail. The rocks on the banks of the creek were frozen in place, secured by hardened mud. The water was frozen, thick enough to support my weight, creating a smooth tabletop interrupted regularly by chunks of churned ice, driftwood and soil. My mind couldn't help drifting back to the story of Jesson as he prepared for his trip more than 100 years before. The Yukon River was a far cry from this modest fingerling of a creek, but as my fat bike found a path through the ice, for the first time I could understand what drove Jesson. Riding a bike up a frozen waterway would never be easy, not with a modern bike engineered for winter like I was riding, and especially with a primitive tubeless single-speed like Jesson rode. But it just might be possible. As I looked up the creek, my mind naturally picking out a path around the obstacles nature laid down, my image of Jesson as a crazy dreamer dissipated. Maybe he was onto something.

CHAPTER 6

My experiment with fat-biking ended up being a little short-lived. While I had great fun on my recreational ride, and fat-biking is something I intend to keep as part of my winter weekend plans (I joined a fat-biking group online, and now read with envy about other dads' overnight bike trips into the bush with their fat-biking kids in the middle of February), but I found the fat bike didn't quite work on my commute. The qualities that make them so great on snow and ice turned out to be a liability when I was rushing to work. The balloon tires seemed to absorb too much energy to keep my speed up. Even after pumping the tires full of air – one of the nice things about a fat bike is the way tire air pressure can change to accommodate different riding conditions – the bike was just too inefficient as a commuter. I see an increasing number of people riding them to work occasionally, and the feeling of safety on snow and ice is a big draw for many, but on my long commute, speed was crucial. I reluctantly returned the fat bike to the store that had lent it to me, sadly envisioning all the melting snow forts in the neighbourhood that I wouldn't be able to crush on a whim. I was back on the hunt for the perfect winter commuting ride.

My next attempt at finding that perfection came from an unlikely place. I had picked up an inexpensive city bike one summer as a means of getting around the neighbourhood. The goal was a low-maintenance, comfortable ride to hit the grocery store for milk, ride to the library with the kids, or, in a best-case scenario, use it to get to the neighbourhood pub. It was a straightforward, inexpensive three-speed cruiser bike, built with simplicity in mind. It had internal gears that negated the need to fiddle with derailleurs, coaster brakes that require next to no maintenance, and a comfortable seat and handlebar alignment that should be of good use when I retire in 30 years with a bad back. In some ways, it was a North American version of the simple machines I kept reading about in European cities such as Copenhagen and Amsterdam, where seemingly everybody rides a cheap, uncomplicated bike, not for fitness or recreation, but simply to get around. I added some fenders and a hauling rack in the back, and the bike proved its mettle within days of getting it home in the middle of summer when I was able to carry home a mini-keg of beer from the neighbour-hood micro-brewery.

I had always planned on putting the bike into storage for the winter, but plans changed. What I liked best about the bike was that it didn't require anything special. I wore no special clothing, and I needed no specialized bike shoes. In fact, I needed nothing. I just hopped on and rode. I enjoyed this so much that I started riding it to work in the summer on occasion. The bike was slow, so I didn't ride it every day, but if I had an offsite meeting down-town, I would often take it to work because I could hop on and beat the car traffic without having to change my clothes. I would show up at my meetings dressed professionally five minutes before my col-leagues, while sneaking in a bonus ride on a lovely summer day. I still liked my regular bike on most days because it got me to the office and gave me a workout at the same time, thus avoiding the dreaded gym, but I would arrive in need of a shower, clad in athletic gear and was forced to embarrassingly click-clack through the office until I could change out of my cycling shoes. Still, having two bike options in the summer was a treat.

There was one problem with Slow Ride, as I af-fectionately named the bike (usually accompanied by the Foghat riff ringing through my brain). In my city, such a bike made me an anomaly. Europeans don't think twice when they see a grown man on an upright, comfortable bike, but to North Americans, at least those in my sphere, and mostly men, tended to wrinkle their noses. Bikes, to most North Americans, are for jocks. You either attack backcountry mountain bike trails wearing body armour and return home bloodied and muddied with a tale to brag about, or you force yourself into absurdly long rides on windswept rural highways on a road bike, and return with another tale to brag about. Bikes are rarely seen simply as a mode of transportation. And if they were, that upright posture tended to be a sign, for some reason, of a girl's bike. That's how I found myself defending Slow Ride at every opportunity. It wasn't just a question of novelty; it was a question of manhood, which was absurd considering how practical and useful the bike proved to be. I had to justify the bike to nearly all my male friends, who wondered aloud why I was riding a bike built for a woman, even if it wasn't. Most accepted my explanations with a look that said, "Whatever, dude," but it was a small price to pay. I came to love riding the bike, and would come up with needless errands to run, just to be given a chance to use it.

Come winter, however, I found myself stalling on my plan to put the bike into storage. Why not give it a whirl in the winter? As a cold-season ride, it had a few things going for it. Its simplicity meant it didn't have many parts to collect grit and snow. Its internal hub protected the gearing from the elements, so it would require less maintenance. What was the problem?

My first winter ride with it was as perfect a ride as you can have in the winter. I bundled up, not with my usual synthetics and sweat-wicking athletic gear, but with an extra layer beneath my pea coat, a stylish scarf, mittens and a toque, the same way I would have done had I taken the bus that day. I looked good, which was a nice improvement over my normal bike-commute look: like a stealth-headed alien en route to a snowball fight. The morning cold disappeared a few minutes into my ride, and I actually had to slow down and remove some of those layers so that I didn't sweat too much. The ride home in the dark was one of those blissful evenings that most people miss in winter because they are hibernating. Large, dry flakes of snow tumbled from the sky and melted as they hit the road, and the night was lit up with sparking crystal reflections. My slower pace gave me more time to enjoy the journey, and I arrived home vowing to make this my new winter ritual.

The next day, however, those wet streets had frozen, and I nearly slid under a parked car before I had reached the end of my street. I returned home and put my usual winter bike, complete with studded tires, back into use. Soon, I was back to my fast, sweaty commute, and I only employed Slow Ride a few more times that winter. I wasn't unhappy with that change. My regular ride turned out just fine and gave me a good workout to boot, but I couldn't help thinking about Slow Ride often. Could Slow Ride become my perfect winter bike? With a few changes, I think it could. Some hardier, all-season tires would fix most of her deficiencies, perhaps some knobby mountain bike tires, or even studded versions. Beyond that, the most significant changes required would have to come from within me. I would have to give up the notion that winter cycling was something exceptional and athletic. I would need to stop that morning ritual of gearing up like a montage from an '80s action movie. I would have to do away with the idea of my commute doubling as extreme exercise. Yet all of those are easy changes and would, in fact, make my life as a cyclist easier. What was I waiting for?

As the season wore on, however, something else emerged that challenged my winter commuting. It also challenged my ideas about the perfect winter bike.

CHAPTER 7

By the end of my first season of winter cycling, I had learned a lot, but I still felt like I didn't have a definitive answer to my big question about the viability of winter cycling. In fact, everything I had learned complicated the question. The easy answer was: yes, riding a bike in the winter is a reasonable thing to do, because I had done it. Spring was approaching, and I was still managing to get out on my bike several days a week. I was enjoying myself in the same way I did during the summer, with the added bonus of having my co-workers think of me as either a head case or impervious to pain. But as the season came to an end, a new problem had emerged.

As winter waned, my bike was staring at me with wounded eyes, pleading for a respite. Winter was taking its toll. The cogs, gummed with slush, rusted and complained about every gearshift. The brakes, after months of being caked with a unique winter kind of slop, made up of mud, snow, salt and sand, grew slack and lazy. The cables stretched, rusted and started to wilt. The seat post warped with corrosion. At that point, with growing horror about what I had done, I belatedly started cleaning my reliable old girl-purple Raleigh after each commute. With the garden hose frozen up, I was forced to trudge into my kitchen and fill a bucket with warm tap water and then go to work with a brush in the backyard. But it was too little, too late. As spring approached, she refused to shift.

Then, on one cold grey day as winter reared its head one of its final times that year, I walked into my garage with a heavy heart. I stripped the Raleigh of all her components, thinking I would save the frame for another season, and reinvigorate the bike with fresh parts. I removed the brakes, which by now squeezed with no resistance. Off came the shifters, the derailleur and the bar ends that had adorned her for more than a decade. As each part came off, the Raleigh seemed to breathe a sigh of relief. She may have another season in her after all. My hope slowly returned.

Then, tragedy struck. The seat post had to be removed and replaced because it was dangerously corroded, but it wouldn't budge. It had rusted in place. I heated the post with a torch. I tried cutting it off with a hacksaw. I pounded it with a hammer. No dice.

Like an old couple who couldn't imagine life without each other, the frame and seat post had made a pact to stick together until the end. I gave them a moment of privacy together, took a photograph for posterity, and then marched them out to the back lane. I placed the frame and welded seat post in the garbage bin and slowly closed the lid on a bike I had grown to love despite its girlish hue. With spring came a new fair-weather bike for me. Throughout the winter, I made a pact with myself to sock away all the money saved by riding to work rather than driving. I even came up with a formula, using my rather limited math skills. If you're trying to convince yourself (or, more importantly, your spouse), that you deserve a new bike, here's what I did. I looked up the fuel consumption of my motor vehicle on the website of the Canadian government's Department of Natural Resources. The average yearly cost of my minivan was estimated at $2,058. I still drove the vehicle on evenings and weekends and occasionally to work when I had to attend out-of-bike-range appointments, but I estimated that bicycle commuting had cut my driving at least in half, if not more. Add insurance, registration, parking fees and the cost of the vehicle, and I came up with a estimation of the amount of money I had saved for every kilometre I rode my bike for transportation (including the cost of the vehicle was cheating a bit because we didn't sell a vehicle when I started riding. And don't ask me for a breakdown of the rest of the figures because I tended to round up because, really, the whole exercise was just to justify a new bike, and I wanted a nice one). So after about a year of riding, including all my winter bicycle commutes, I had enough to hit the spring sale at my local bike shop and buy a nice new Specialized Tricross, a good quality cyclocross bike. Cyclocross is a style of off-road racing that takes place on short courses in which competitors occasionally dismount and leap over obstacles while carrying their bikes, usually in the mud. A cyclocross bike was a nice option for me because it is a little tougher and sturdier than a pure road bike, but was still speedy and light, perfect for longer commutes like mine. And with a second set of smooth tires, I could even hit the roads for some longer weekend rides.

Despite the pain of losing my Raleigh, I quickly fell in love with the Specialized. The bike was speedy and tough, and I babied it shamelessly. Soon, in addition to my commuting, I was doing long fitness rides through the rolling foothills of the Rockies and signing up for 140-kilometre group rides. I was a totally new kind of cyclist, and I loved it.

But all that summer, winter loomed over my bike rides like a distant storm cloud. I knew it was coming, and considering the way winter had manhandled my Raleigh, there was no way I was going to subject my new bike to the season's destructiveness. I needed another bike specifically for the snow and ice. I needed a winter bike.

For a while, I considered my options. The previous winter's experiences had opened my eyes to a world of two-wheeled winter machines that I hadn't know existed, but I wasn't sure any were right for me. A fat bike, I determined, was great for recreation – I'm convinced bombing down snow-covered hills on five-inch tires will be in the Winter Olympics some day – but it wasn't quite right for my commute. Sure, I would be able to power over powder, but with most of my commute taking place on at least marginally maintained city roads and pathways, a fat bike wasn't a perfect fit. What it offered me in safety and pure joy couldn't make up for its sluggishness on roads. Likewise, the Hanebrink would be my go-to mode if I ever decide to bicycle to the North Pole or across the Sahara with an empty wallet, but it didn't feel fit for my commute.

For a while, I considered Slow Ride, or an all-season European bike. It seemed like it would fit the bill, and I had little doubt that it could survive a Canadian winter. But I relied on it so much in summer that I wasn't keen to gamble on ruining it with rust in the winter. And buying a new bike was not in the cards. Call me cheap (many do), but one of the great things about using a bike as a primary mode of transportation is the cost savings. Forking out for two new rides in one calendar year seemed extravagant. At least that's what my wife told me. So I was stumped. After all I'd learned about finding the perfect winter bike, I was more confused than ever.

Around that time, I was taking the long way to work one lovely day when I came across a mobile bike mechanic. You've probably seen these guys in your city. A mechanic stocks a work van with tools, parks near a busy bicycle commuter route headed into downtown and picks up all the tune-up traffic from cyclists too busy to hit bricks-and-mortar bike shops. They are food trucks for bikes. It was a sunny summer afternoon and, even though I didn't need any work done on my bike, I stopped in and started chatting. The mechanic was one of those veterans of life who oozed a world-weary kind of coolness, as if he'd seen everything in the world and was unfazed by all of it. After a while of chatting, he gave up trying to get rid of me, set out two lawn chairs, lit a cigarette, and we sat down.

Joe recounted a few of his bicycle stories. He was no specialist; he had done it all: racing, touring, working as a bike courier. He had bought his truck a couple of years before, and had managed to make a decent seasonal living tuning up the expensive bikes of downtown commuters who couldn't be bothered to lube their own chain. He pondered what to do in the winter to earn a living – mobile ski tune-ups, perhaps? – which brought the conversation around to my winter bike conundrum. When I told him I was considering buying a bike specifically for winter, he looked at me as if I was crazy. Don't spend good money on a winter bike, he said. It's futile. You need a P.O.S. for winter. When I sheepishly asked him what a P.O.S. was, he sucked a drag from his cigarette and exhaled into the sky. "Piece of shit," he said. "The perfect winter bike is one that costs nothing. Single speed, maybe a fixie. Disc brakes. Make it simple. You're going to trash it anyway, so why spend a lot of money on it?"

When I left Joe, his brutal logic started to sink in. Maybe he was right. Maybe the perfect winter bike wasn't an over-engineered, balloon-tired piece of art. In some other cities, winter bikes don't rust. Keeping a bike in the cold all season long does tend to preserve it in some places. But the relentless freeze-melt cycle of my city was forcing me to think creatively. Was I taking the wrong approach?

The next week, I stopped by one of the city's community bike shops, a place set up by young, idealistic community organizers as a drop-in DIY bike service stop, usually bedecked with homeless men truing their tires. I had used the shop occasionally over the years when I needed a quick fix with a special bike tool that I didn't own, and I knew the store put an ever-changing pile of castoff bikes up for grabs for next to nothing. I combed through a menagerie of refurbished ten-speeds and seatless kids' mountain bikes with suspension, and was about to give up when I saw it. Like a well-behaved Labrador in a puppy mill, she was just lying there staring at me, waiting to be discovered. I pulled a few frames off of her, and lifted her out for a closer look. She was an orange Specialized Rockhopper, at least 15 years old I guessed, maybe 20, missing her tires, her cables loose and dangling, and her saddle turned backwards and torn. The frame, however, was solid, other than a few scratches, and was built of rust-resistant aluminum. Overall, she looked like teenaged Dickensian orphan, who had long ago given up the hope of finding a home, but carried a beautiful face beneath the grime. Such orphans hold such promise, but also the potential to ruin both of our lives. But there was one thing about her I couldn't resist. The price: a lowly $50.

Over the coming weeks, as the days grew shorter, I began to winterize my new ride. I had some old wheels and some knobby tires in my garage that I cleaned up and mounted, reserving my homemade studded tires for when the slippery conditions truly set in. I installed new brake cables. I took Joe's advice and stripped off all unnecessary parts, including the shifters and derailleurs. I bought a $10 conversion kit and turned the bike into a single speed freewheel, in the process dropping the back cassette which, on my old bike, was a magnet for debilitating salted slush. I bought some cheap fenders to keep my butt dry, and powerful back and front lights to get me through the dark mornings. After chipping away at the project over a couple of weeks, I stepped back in assessment. I had put a minimal amount of work into the bike – installing winter tires on my car probably took more time – and for less than $100, I was feeling pretty good about my first real winter bicycle. And if the experiment flopped, at least I hadn't broken the bank. Snow came early that year and, for the first time since I was a kid, I was excited by it. I pulled on my long johns and hit the roads early. The snow hadn't been cleared from the roads or pathways, and I hadn't developed my winter balance yet, which is the two-wheeled equivalent of sea legs, so it was a wobbly ride. Early on, I spotted another bicycle commuter mounted on a nice all-season European-style bike, which boasted an internal belt drive and a light powered by the riders' pedalling. As he effortlessly downshifted his way up a slight embankment and I struggled behind with no option of shifting, pangs of envy coursed through me. But over the rest of my ride, I noticed the roads filled with other P.O.S.'s. Some were, like mine, outfitted for winter, but many were simply crappy old garage fillers that had been resurrected for winter. As I cruised along the steaming river, I had one of those moments that I love about cycling. My movements had warmed my body completely, I cruised past lines of cars trapped in traffic, the sky around them obscured by a thousand steaming tailpipes, and my endorphins had kicked in making me feel like I could ride forever. Sure, a nice all-season bike would be great, but maybe Lance Armstrong was right. Maybe it's not about the bike.

That day made me think back to the Klondike gold rusher Edward Jesson, and that day he kicked off his 1200 kilometre journey across Alaska, at a time before roads, in the dead of winter, on a rudimentary bike he had started riding only a week previously.

The early days of the journey were not easy for Jesson, according to his journals. Despite his enthusiasm about riding a bicycle all the way from Dawson City to Nome on frozen rivers, he had a backup plan – Jesson managed to convince a fellow gold rusher to follow behind in a dogsled, although the fate of the dogsled is never mentioned in his journals. On the first day on the trail with his bicycle, Jesson "took about 25 headers" into the snow, and each time he fell, the dogs trailing behind playfully piled on top of him, and he could only get them back on track by "whipping them unmercifully which would break their spirit and this was the only fun they had all winter." However, he managed to make it to the first of the hundreds of roadhouses that had been established along the trail to feed and shelter gold rushers. The next day was even worse. The temperature on that 23rd of February plummeted to -48 °F. In his diaries, Jesson reserves most of his complaining for his compatriot's fair-weather attitude, but does note that the bike wasn't faring so well in such cold either. "The rubber tires on my wheel were frozen hard and stiff as gass [sic] pipe. The oil in my bearings was frozen and I could scarcely ride it and my nose was freezing and I had to hold the handlebars with both hands not being able to ride yet with one hand and rub my nose with the other."

Soon, however, things improved. On most days, Jesson found that he could cover up to 65 kilometres a day on his bicycle, even on ice full of cracks and side-slopes that threatened to push him into the snow banks. On his bicycle, he outpaced even the best dogsleds. On good days, in fact, Jesson recalled passing dozens of sleds, no doubt piloted by bewildered mushers scratching their heads over the pace of this bizarre "wheelman." By March, Jesson had come to love his new contraption, especially after one unusually horrendous day on the ice. The trail was inexplicably broken up, which confounded Jesson and made for the "hardest riding I have seen." He struggled along until he came upon a preacher and his companion making the trip with two sledge-hauling horses who kept breaking through the rough ice, leaving the animals' feet bleeding and the sleds lurching all over the trail, causing even more damage to the ice. This made the river nearly impassable. The stampeders following behind bore the brunt of this folly. The shards of ice that littered the river caused men to trip and sprain ankles, and the sharp edges sliced mercilessly into the feet of the dogs. "The trail was bloody for miles from the bleeding and limping dogs," Jesson wrote. "What those dog men said and thought about the 2 men and horses would burn up a ton of asbestos fireproof paper." Jesson, however, managed to pass the horsemen unscathed. "I was never more pleased with my wheel than when I passed them about 3:40 that afternoon and the wheel was still in good condition," he wrote.

For several more weeks, Jesson cruised toward Nome, constantly fielding questions from curious onlookers, and demonstrating the bicycle to groups of fascinated First Nations people along the way, one of whom offered him $150 on the spot to buy the bike. Jesson declined. Not all gold-rush cyclists had such luck. Max Hirschberg, who made the trip in 1900, suffered snow blindness and nearly drowned after falling through the ice (he lost $1,500 of gold dust in the process). Others saw their handlebars break in the cold, which they fixed by fashioning new ones from tree branches. Still others managed to make good time by jury-rigging their coats into sails that were pushed along by the winter wind.

For his part, Jesson ended his journals with a parenthetical statement that seemed almost like an afterthought, but has stuck with me through my own winter rides. My own bike held up quite well for that first winter, and, in fact, I'm still riding it, several years later. On those dark winter mornings when the endorphins don't leave me feeling giddy, and I'm feeling a little sorry for myself when that dude with the beautiful Euro-model cruises past me on the uphills, I remember that final statement Jesson left in his journal, a judgment, not only on his own crude bicycle, but on the viability of winter cycling in general: "The wheel stood the trip in splendid shape and to my great surprise I never had a puncture or broke a spoke the entire trip."

After all the challenges I faced during my first winter, I thought more about the question that drove me in the first place. Despite a few setbacks, I realized that what's holding most of us back from winter cycling may not, in fact, be the bike. Of all the bikes I tried, none of them were complete failures. With a few modifications, I'm convinced just about any bike could get happily through a winter. Adding some studded tires, some fenders and regular cleanings can work wonders. To think otherwise is to discount what Jesson experienced more than 100 years ago. We live in an era of specialization, when the right tool for a job isn't right unless it's perfect.

In a different era, Jesson proved that good enough could work out just as well. Perhaps my search for the perfect winter bike was misguided. If something is holding us back from embracing winter cycling, it may not be the lack of the perfect bike. So what is it?

It dawned on me that my search for the consummate machine was focusing on the symptom, rather than the problem. During those times when winter riding wasn't an image of bliss, and there were many of them, my biggest hurdles were things beyond my control. I struggled with unplowed streets, icy pathways and unpleasant drivers. The things that make urban cycling a challenge in the summer – cyclists are often forced to exist in the seams of our urban infrastructure, squeezed between pedestrians and motorists and the infrastructure built for them – are exponentially worse in the winter. If I felt squeezed on a road in the summer, it was worse in winter when snowbanks would eat up road shoulders. If a road lacked a bike lane in summer, the need for one increased in winter when the chances of slipping beneath a nearby car grew. The more research I did into winter cycling, the more I realized these problems were not unique. In fact, every winter city seems to struggle with similar problems.

That simple realization set me off on a new search.

Perhaps what holds us back from embracing winter cycling isn't the bike. Perhaps it's the place.

SEASON TWO
THE CITY

CHAPTER 8

It's a bright, brisk February morning, about –9°c (15°F) the day after a fresh snowfall. Earlier in the week, the temperature burst past the freezing mark, and for a few hours in the afternoon, the accumulated snow broke down under a brilliant winter sun, sending meltwater dripping off rooftops and trickling into storm drains. As the sun went down, however, the temperature crept back down below 0°c, and the freezing set in. Those rivulets of water criss-crossing roads and sidewalks stopped, fixed in place as if waiting for unsuspecting passersby. To make things worse, the subsequent snowfall hid those danger spots.

Into this I pushed off on my bike. Finally, I was riding a winter machine I was happy with, that old aluminum-framed mountain bike converted down to a single speed. It wasn't perfect – the single speed slowed me down and was murder on big hills – but four months into winter, the machine was holding up, staving off rust and keeping me moving, and upright, through the snow.

By this point into winter, my winter bike-riding commute had gone so well that I had developed a routine. I knew how to dress for different temperatures, I trusted my bike, and myself, on the snow, and I had mapped out a new route to work that was effective. It was different than my summer course because I was forced to abandon some bike pathways that weren't plowed and use more city streets. It made for a slightly more lengthy ride, and with my slower pace, my winter commute took longer than in summer, but I was managing to commute by bike a few times a week. I was enjoying it. I didn't realize it at the time, but I was even starting to get a little cocky.

Normally, riding through a fresh snowfall is an invigorating experience. There seems to be some primal human need to leave fresh tracks. It feels good, in a childlike way, like jumping into a puddle, or squishing worms on the sidewalk after a rain. On this day, however, leaving fresh tracks was a journey into the unknown. Within moments of kicking off down the road, I realized the snow was hiding spots of ice, and a wobbly stop at the end of my street sent my heart into my throat. I told myself to slow down, and take the safest path on every road. By now, city work crews had plowed the major routes, but those plows had left windrows of dirty snow on the shoulders of roads, which was exactly where I ride. Rather than travel over these piles of snow, an impossibility, I heeded the old advice doled out by veteran urban cyclists and "took the lane" – instead of cowering over in the gutter lane, I rode in the middle of the street where it was plowed. Doing so, however, put me in the path of impatient motorists, and soon there was a line of cars building up behind me.

I drive a car, so I know how frustrating obstacles are, especially when that obstacle is a cyclist too obstinate to put his bike away in the winter. So as the number of cars built up behind me, I could practically feel their irritation rising. I tried moving over, but as soon as I hit the plowed snow, my back tire shook and slid. I imagined it flying out from under me, grinding under the wheels of a moving vehicle, as the driver gleefully accelerates over me like a speed bump. Unnerved, I went back to the middle of the road. I was rewarded with an angry pickup truck driver who blazed past me with only a few precious inches of clearance.

That was enough for me. At the next intersection, I turned off in search of a parallel but less busy route. I wound up on a residential street that was indeed less lousy with commuting vehicles, but hadn't been plowed yet. I enjoyed the less murderous pace here, but a new danger emerged. With no plowing, the few vehicles that had gone down this road had packed down the snow into a smooth grey compress that looked stable until my tires touched it. Then, it would give way like sand, revealing glistening ice below. It was a trap, and it was too late to turn back.

My bike lurched from side to side atop this deadly concoction, and I stayed upright only through luck. But a car had come up behind me and I was fast approaching a T-intersection. On this amalgam of snow and ice, brakes were the tipping point. As I squeezed the levers, my back tire slowly but unstoppably went its own way, taking the bike from under me. I hit the ground on my side, and slowly slid to a rest at the stop sign. I was unhurt, but as I lay on the ground for a moment I had an interesting vantage point. The face of the driver behind me showed concern (but not enough concern to actually help), and I realized the crossroad on the other side of the stop sign was a freshly plowed collector route that had been sanded and salted and ready for all manner of vehicles. That's when a bike commuter, decked out in layered Lycra and studded tires, swiftly rode by on that sanded road, and as he passed, he looked down on me in confusion, wondering why, in God's name, I was lying on the snow in the middle of the road.

As I lay there, falling snow slowly accumulating on my prone body, that old nagging question came back to me. Sure, I had finally found a winter bike that was working for me, but maybe there was more to riding a bike in the winter than finding the perfect machine. Maybe I also needed the perfect city.

CHAPTER 9

In the mid-1990s, Colynn Kerr was a municipal worker in Calgary, and a bit of a bike buff. He was part of a small but dedicated group of commuters at the time who used their bikes to get to work. Luckily for Kerr, he lived only a few kilometres outside of downtown near a paved pathway, built for walkers and cyclists, that snaked along the Bow River from the suburbs all the way into the city's core.

The pathway system in Calgary, like many urban pathway networks in North America, traced its origins back to the bicycle revival of the 1970s. By then, cars had completed their takeover of cities all over the world, while bikes had slowly and steadily fallen from their position as a vehicle of transportation at the turn of the 20th century to nothing more than toys for kids. By the 1970s, however, a number of factors came together to return cycling to the world of adults.

First, there was the fitness craze of the era. Fuelled, in the U.S. by the rock-star status of athletes such as runner Steve Prefontaine, in Canada by an athletic prime minister in Pierre Trudeau, and a much disseminated report that shamed North Americans into the realization that Swedish senior citizens were in better shape than they were, North Americans started getting off the couch to tie on running shoes and hit the gym for Jazzercise and aerobics classes. At the same, the oil crisis drove gas prices skyward and the nascent environmental movement suggested, for the first time for many people, that cars might be bad. The result: by the early 1970s, bike sales doubled in some areas of North America, even outselling cars in the U.S. for the first time in decades.

In some cities, the response to this craze was the creation of the first wave of recreational bike paths. In Minnesota, the Heartland State Trail, a 79-kilometre paved route along an abandoned rail line, was created by the state legislature in 1974. In Canada, several cities started building recreational bike paths, which began as simple red shale routes in many areas that were later paved when they proved popular. These weren't the kind of segregated on-street paths being built in many North American cities today – bike advocacy at the time was dominated by activist John Forester's concepts around "vehicular cycling," which encouraged cyclists to ride on roads as if they were vehicles, based on the idea they would fare better if they were treated equally by drivers. As such, bike lanes were rarely seen as necessary. What were being built were lazy routes through parks intended for Sunday family rides.

In Calgary, a network of such pathways continued to be built through the 1980s and '90s, and even though many of the paths featured long, indirect routes between destinations, many cyclists took to them in early mornings as commuting routes because they were safer than jostling with cars on roads. Kerr lived just off one such pathway that took him downtown to city hall, and he soon found himself among a small group of regular bicycle commuters.

Come every winter, however, the first snowfall put an end to bicycle commuting for most people. The pathways were not plowed, so it was impossible to get a bike through the snow. So Kerr, like most others, hung up his bike for the season and reluctantly started using his car and public transit. But he didn't like it. He missed his daily bike ride.

So one day, he had an idea. He found a big plastic pail and cut it in two. He built a frame in the shape of a triangle using some leftover lumber, and screwed the rounded plastic sides of the pail to the frame. He weighed the whole contraption down with an empty plastic Coke bottle filled with sand, and using some rope, tied it to the back of his mountain bike. He brought the whole thing to the pathway and started riding, with his prototype dragging behind. Just like he hoped, as he rode through the snow, his construction cut through the snow behind, leaving a patch of clear asphalt a few feet wide. He had built a rudimentary plow that could be dragged behind his bike. A DIY pathway plow.

Eventually, Kerr attracted a bit of a following, and a small group of cyclists had honed his design, and began attacking the pathways after every snowfall. In the evenings, as the snow was falling, the volunteer group would bundle up, make their way to the pathways and start plowing. "I couldn't believe how well it worked," one of those members, Jeff Gruttz told me over coffee, 20 years later. "In light snow, before it was packed, it did a great job."

It wasn't a huge group of people, but they were zealous. They worked out a deal with city hall that allowed them to do the work on a municipal asset, and soon, commuters and recreationalists noticed the cleared pathways and returned. Dressed in ski jackets and scarves, riding mountain bikes with knobby tires and studs, the first waves of winter bike commuters was finally able to keep it up year-round. The volunteer snow-removal corps eventually expanded their plowing area to several kilometres of routes outside the downtown core, even retrofitting Gruttz's old Datsun pickup truck with a bigger plow that brought a little internal-combustion muscle to the job. The local newspaper wrote about the group as a novelty, as did a national newsweekly magazine: a bunch of kooks who didn't know when to put their bikes away. Wire services sent the story around the country, and Gruttz recalled getting a call from his bemused sister in Vancouver, excited about his moment of fame, but a little mystified that he would spend his cold winter evenings clearing snow so other people could ride bicycles.

There was little such soul-searching among the volunteer plowers. They saw the impact of their work. For five years, the volunteers cleared snow, bringing to the pathways a core group of commuters and weekend recreationalists who would otherwise be on the couch or clogging up roads in their vehicles on the way to work. They felt they were making the city better. It was difficult, but gratifying work. But then, something happened that changed everything.

In was St. Patrick's Day in 1993, and a massive snowstorm hit the city; the worst March storm in

113 years, according to Environment Canada. The city was socked with a huge pile of wet spring snow, as much as 45 centimetres (17 inches) in some areas. Everyone, it seemed, huddled into their homes and waited out the storm, and its aftermath, except, of course, for the volunteer pathway clearing crew.

Gruttz recalled being behind the wheel of his Datsun in the hours after the storm. The snow was so deep the plow couldn't penetrate. When it did cut its way through, snow poured over the top of the plow, burying it and rendering it useless. He recruited two volunteers to stand on the edges of the plow while he drove, to weigh it down and to clear snow as it spilled over the top, as if bailing water from a sinking raft. But it wasn't enough. The snow proved too much. For the first time since Kerr pieced together that initial bike path plow, the group gave up.

Something unexpected happened next. Legions of cyclists and walkers who had become accustomed to using the pathways started phoning city hall with complaints. Why haven't you cleared the pathways yet? What's taking so long? The volunteers had become so good at their job that pathway users assumed municipal employees were being paid to do the work. Not realizing that a group of volunteers was behind it, they called to chastise City Hall for the failure. That day was a turning point. Kerr later recalled that those complaints made City Hall realize that people needed pathways all year long. A public hearing into the matter brought out hundreds of walkers, joggers and cyclists to demand expanded snow clearing. Kerr recalled an old blind man with a Scottish accent chiding city council over its failure to plow more pathways, saying he was liable to wander out onto the river ice if he couldn't find the edge of the path plowed into the snow.

That day kicked off an expanded pathway snow clearing system that slowly grew until many of the major pathways in the city were factored into the snow-clearing budget. By the time I started commuting in the winter a decade later, the pathways were routinely cleared of snow before many roads. It still isn't a perfect system – not all pathways are plowed, and not all are great for commuting – but my daily trip to work involves paths for about a third of the distance, and it is, on most days, the least harrowing part of the ride.

As I started thinking more about winter cycling, the story of Calgary's pathway plowing became a kind of metaphor for something bigger. As I talked with people in other cities about cycling in the winter, I was amazed at the discrepancies. Some cities poured money into winter maintenance to make cycling easy year round. Others did nothing. Some cities that had made summer cycling a priority were surprisingly lax in the winter – after spending millions constructing bike lanes, some cities actually used the lanes in the winter as a place to store snow that had been removed from roads.

. In seeking an answer to my big question about the feasibility of winter cycling on a large scale, what I found was a patchwork of ideas and plans around urban winter cycling that turned out to be just as important to winter cyclists as the bicycle itself. And perhaps most importantly, I found the model city, a semi-mythical place on the other side of the world that showed me just how viable cycling in the winter can be.

CHAPTER 10

The world's biggest conference on urban cycling took over two floors of the Sheraton Vancouver Wall Centre Hotel. It was 2012, and Velo-City, the world's foremost international conference on urban cycling rolled into North America for the first time in a decade. At this point, I had started a bike blog at the newspaper I was working at, posting a few times a week during my down time, and this conference seemed like a way to learn more about urban cycling, and bag a few blog postings along the way. So I convinced my editor to give me a couple of days off, made the short hop to Vancouver, and entered a new world.

The conference brought earnest bike lovers from all over the globe to share ideas about making cities friendlier to cyclists. There were city planners in cheap golf shirts stuffing their canvas bags with freebies. Environmentalists with greying beards chatted with young urban planning graduates. Trim European urbanists chuckled at all the cyclists wearing helmets.

In the big conference room in the basement, rock stars of the cycling world delivered powerhouse speeches of inspiration to thousands of believers. For a North American like me, where bikes are, in most cities, still considered toys for kids and jocks, the bike's importance in other cities was eye opening. What's more, the petty arguments about the benefits of the bike that serve as a prelude to every discussion about cycling back at home were nowhere – here, everyone accepted that bikes are cheap and fast, good for one's health and the environment, beneficial to street life, and they help unclog congested roads. These debates were a step beyond. It wasn't a question about whether cycling can make cities better. It was a question of how we can enable it to happen.

During a keynote address, Gil Penalosa, the former parks commissioner of Bogota, Colombia, who became famous building bike lanes in the city's *favelas*, chastised North American cities for dragging their feet on the implementation of bike lanes. "We are still at the beginning of this movement," he thundered like a street preacher. "We have the momentum." With a tone that was part pleading and part rabble-rousing, he scolded timid urban planners for not moving quickly enough on building bike lanes segregated from cars, comparing piecemeal bike infrastructure to building half a soccer pitch and then complaining nobody uses it. "Don't bother with painted lanes," he cried. "If you fight and fight and fight for a bike lane that doesn't work, it's a step backwards because people who don't like cycling say 'See! They don't work.'" You could practically hear the minds of North American bureaucrats, beaten down by careers spent battling red tape and reactionary anti-cycling sentiment, being blown.

Throughout the conference, there were panel discussions about integrating bike lanes and public transit. I sat in on passionate debates about the need for bike helmets, an argument between those armed with stories of saved brains and others who point out studies that find "plastic hats" discourage bicycle use and don't work very well in saving lives either. In small conference rooms, researchers presented studies on the best ways of making public bike-sharing schemes work, and how to get more kids riding their bikes to school. I met an Australian living in Belgium who complained that North Americans erroneously think European cities are naturally friendly to bikes, as if the cities were born with bike lanes and something everybody likes to call "bike culture." "Come to Brussels," he said to me, a little bitterly. "It's terrible for bikes." I ran into a civil servant from Copenhagen that I had once interviewed for a story I wrote. He was trying to lie low this week, but every time I saw him, he was being peppered with questions by people trying to learn how his home city had managed to become a haven for bikes over the past 30 years.

After a couple of days at the conference, I picked up on some of the unique vocabulary that has evolved in gatherings such as this. There was even a distinctive style of greeting. When people met, they would say their name, their city, and their city's modal share, which means the percentage of commuters who use each transportation mode, in this case bikes, to get to work. North Americans tended to say their modal share sheepishly and apologetically. Europeans said it with feigned modesty, a kind of international humblebrag, like this: "Hi, I'm Tom. I'm from Calgary, Canada. Yeah, our modal share is only about 2 per cent, but we've got a really nice pathway system." "Hello, Tom. I'm Sven, from Malmö, Sweden. We only have about 30 per cent. It should be much higher. But, you know, all those people with their cars." Sometimes it feels like speed dating. "Ooh, 4 per cent modal share in a North American city? You must be doing something right. Maybe you could tell me about it over drinks later?"

In the middle of the conference, as I thumbed my

way through the program, I spotted a mention of a small roundtable discussion centred around the idea of winter. I was a little taken aback. In four days of talks about cycling, this was the first mention of winter I had heard. I finished my sandwich and headed off to check out this mysterious discussion about snow in a city that rarely sees it.

I walked past hundreds of presenters hawking everything from traffic-counting contraptions to bike racks and out the lobby entrance, past hundreds of bikes brought in for delegates to borrow, and into a neighbouring building. Up an escalator I went, and through some doors far from the main conference area. I was sure I was lost when I found a door to a small conference room ajar. I slipped inside and saw a half-dozen people crowded around a small table filled with paper and half-empty glasses of tap water. This was it. This was the totality of discussions about winter cycling at the biggest bicycle conference in the world; a motley crew of outsiders and bureaucrats, made up of at least one person wearing woollen socks with sandals, a few municipal workers specializing in snow plowing, and a few Scandinavians teasing each other about the severity of their winter. An American cycling advocate from Denver talked about the types of clothing she likes to wear while riding a bike in winter. Someone else talked about the type of plow blades that work best on bike paths. They joked about the reactions they receive when they discuss winter cycling, even at this conference filled with cycling advocates, which range from disbelief to flabbergasted.

I was about to give up on the discussion as unproductive when, after a long talk about road salt, the floor was turned over to a slight, grey-haired and bespectacled man whom I hadn't noticed previously. He cleared his throat, and in a quiet voice flecked with a Finnish accent, introduced himself as a city bureaucrat from a small municipality in northern Finland. "The best winter cycling city in the world," he said softly. This statement caused a bit of a stir in the gathered crowd, skeptical eyebrows raised. Nobody had ever heard of this city, and this guy was claiming it as the world's best? Suddenly, everybody was paying attention. Who is this guy, I wondered, and where is he from? I discreetly turned to my program, which had precious little information. Jaakko Ylinampa from Oulu, Finland. On my smartphone, I checked Google Maps to find a coastal city in northern Finland, just south of the Arctic Circle. Ylinampa started to talk, and everyone at the table leaned in.

Ylinampa went on to describe what sounded

like a fantasyland of winter cycling. A network of bike pathways built up over the past 30 years away from roads, often with shorter, more direct routes than the cars receive. New areas of the city are built with bicycle routes first. Plows clear bike paths before roads. A populace in which up to 22 per cent of the cyclists ride their bikes every day, and a third of those continue to do so year round. With a winter modal share like that, this guy would kill at bicycle bureaucrat speed dating. Ylinampa finished his short presentation by saying he was leaving Oulu to take another job elsewhere, but he was happy to answer questions. The leaned-in crowd straightened in their seats in stunned silence. Then the questions started. "How many of those bike paths are lit by streetlights?" asked somebody obviously familiar with both the short daylight hours of northern winters, and the typical bike route in North America that features no lighting. Ylinampa looked confused, like he had never considered the question before. "All of them," he said, matter-of-factly. There was a gasp from the group, followed by some murmuring. Somebody asked about plowing, and he described a small army of pathway vehicles at the ready to clear the snow. None of that prepared the group for what came next. Ylinampa described a recently completed project that installed underground heating beneath the town square. When it snows, the heat is turned on, melting it away.

This was too much for me. After the winters I had struggled through, and my focus on finding the perfect winter bicycle to get me through the season, this moment taught me there is a whole other factor to winter cycling that I hadn't considered before. We don't ride our bikes in isolation. We ride in cities, and those cities have much influence on the way we ride, especially in the winter. Could cities be built in a way that could make winter cycling easier? Is there the perfect winter-bike city?

Before Ylinampa finished speaking, I knew I had to get to Oulu.

CHAPTER 11

In the early 1980s, a group of North American urban planners and architects who had been bumping into each other at conferences for years realized they were always having the same conversations. This wasn't about suburbanization, which was already being identified as a problem in planning circles, or ghettoization, which had emerged as the ultimate failure of urban planning of the previous 30 years. It wasn't even about the things that normally occupied the minds of such people: the width of roads or population density. It was about weather.

These planners found themselves kvetching about weather in the same knee-jerk way that everybody does, but unlike other people, they thought they could do something about it. They couldn't fix bad weather (although that still hasn't stopped some people from trying; some jurisdictions continue to send airplanes into storm clouds to dump silver iodide in an attempt to reduce the size of hail stones to cut down on the damage caused by them), but they had a crazy notion that they could build cities to make winter a little more manageable.

In 1982, the Livable Winter Cities Association was formed. The group's first conference was held that year, drawing city planners, architects, engineers and outdoor buffs from a number of northern cities together to talk about ways of making city life a little easier in the winter. For more than 20 years, the group held annual conferences and published a quarterly magazine detailing such subjects as maintaining urban plazas when they are covered with snow, ways of reducing the risk of icicle buildup on rooftops, and using trees to reduce the impact of cold winter winds on buildings. It was a small but passionate group, and they marked their victories in small ways: modifications to plows to prevent the buildup of windrows in front-yard driveways; the encouragement of winter festivals; bus shelters that keep out the cold.

The ideas never quite caught on in a mass way. By 2005, when travel in the U.S. became a hassle in the aftermath of 9/11, the group faded away.

One of those members, however, refused to give up. Patrick Coleman, a city planner who lives in Michigan, picked up the mantle. He changed the name of the group to the Winter Cities

Institute, compiled all the information the organization had generated over the years into a website, wintercities.com, and changed its focus from an annual meeting to a year-round resource for northern urbanites. Today, the idea lives on, mostly through the work of Coleman, who posts stories about winter festivals and winter walkability to a few hundred people on a Facebook page, and fields questions from researching grad students. If the idea still hasn't broken through into the mainstream, it isn't from a lack of passion.

A conversation with Coleman is an assumption-defying, eye-opening journey into the ways our cities ignore winter. Planners and engineers, he says, all tend to work as if they live in southern California. Why, for example, is glass used as a major building material in northern cities when winter saps heat through it for six months of the year? Why are buildings constructed without regard to the prevailing winter winds? Why are ledges constructed to shelter people from rain, yet those ledges collect massive buildups of hazardous icicles in the winter? Why can't urban design redirect warming sunshine into areas where people congregate in winter? When you start posing these questions, you can't help but view cities a little differently. After talking with Coleman,

I started noticing things I hadn't before. While walking with my kids past the local playground, I realized it becomes a dead zone for much of the winter. The play structure becomes slippery in the snow, and the climbing bars are useless when wearing mittens. No wonder kids never want to play there in the winter. Why can't the playground be built to make winter fun? How about using materials that are usable in boots and ski jackets? Why not modify landscape in order to encourage sledding? These are the kinds of things that seem to go unnoticed in our denial of winter.

One of Coleman's biggest peeves is how we design cities to avoid winter. Indoor walkways, such as the veritable underground city in Montreal, and the network of walkways between downtown buildings in my own city of Calgary, are convenient, but making it easy to avoid the outdoors has a psychological impact on us. It tends to make winter seem like the enemy. One of the founders of the original Livable Winter Cities Association was an urban planner named Harold Hanen, who is lauded in Calgary as a visionary builder. His biggest contribution was the plus-15 system of elevated walkways between skyscrapers, which enables pedestrians to make their way from one end of downtown to the other without going outside. Hanen envisioned an indoor city, with the equivalent street life you'd find outside. What emerged instead was a network of stale walking routes peppered with corporate retail establishments and fast-food joints. The network is beloved by office workers because they can leave their jackets in the office when going for lunch, but lamented by a new generation of planners for killing street life in the winter. One visiting consultant described such walkways as "vacuums that suck all the life from the streets."

Some of the biggest winter-friendly initiatives that Coleman sees are among the smallest. He likes talking about a simple gate that can be added to snowplows to reduce annoying windrows being left in front of people's property. He loves when cities do things to encourage outdoor recreation in the winter, by clearing snow from frozen ponds or setting cross-country ski tracks through parks. Winter festivals get him especially excited.

Yet, when I bring up the topic of winter cycling with Coleman, the conversation comes to an end. There's not much he has seen anywhere that encourages winter cycling. Most cities shut down their bicycle sharing programs in the winter. Many don't even plow their bikes lanes or pathways. Some even use bike lanes as a place to dump snow removed from roads. Coleman says bicycles could be a viable form of recreation and transportation in the winter, but it would require some work from cities to make it feasible, something that hasn't quite happened in most places. There are a lot of factors that go into making a good winter city, he says, and chief among those is transportation. So what will it take to make bikes part of that?

It takes another bad winter cycling moment to push me into the next step in my journey. During one of Calgary's characteristic mid-winter melts, I'm enjoying the warm wind and the patches of bare pavement that come with it when a reminder of the challenges of winter hits me. In fact, it hits me right in the face. A passing truck throws a big, sloppy mix of melted snow and mud across my cheek and, disgustingly, into my mouth. As I type this I can still recall the taste: a gritty mixture of dirt and brackish grit.

That evening, I dove into Google on a search for the perfect winter cycling city, that semi-mythical Finnish place I had heard about at the bicycle conference the past spring, which now seemed like a distant memory. Oulu existed and, to my delight, I stumbled across a website inviting cyclists to attend the first-ever winter cycling conference that was to be hosted in the city that February. I could hardly believe the serendipity. Here was a chance to see what winter cities were doing to enable winter cycling, in the very place touting itself as the best winter cycling city in the world. I didn't hesitate. I booked a flight to northern Finland for the middle of winter.

CHAPTER 12

It was pitch black, about one a.m., and snow was falling in lazy chunks, illuminated by the lights of the Finnair flight from Helsinki to Oulu. I craned my neck to the window to see what the world's greatest winter cycling city might look like from the air, but it appeared the same as any other snow-covered municipality in winter – a sea of white with pools of orange where street lights reflected off the snow. My airplane was filled with strapping young men wearing badly knotted ties, a group that I instinctively recognized from a lifetime in Canada as a hockey team. I was tentative as the plane descended, not knowing what to expect upon my arrival. My research into the city revealed little, other than it hosted the Air Guitar World Championships every summer. My requests to the organizers of I Bike Oulu, the world's first major winter cycling conference, were greeted with enthusiasm, and I was generously given a spot at the conference as the only visiting foreign journalist. The conference organizer, a man named Timo Perala who, with his wild-eyed Internet profile photo featuring a wayward blond beard, struck me as a half-mad Nordic ski bum (which, thanks to the Nordic penchant for cross-country skiing, made them much fitter than their North American ski bum brethren), seemed excited by the prospect of some coverage in a North American newspaper. Via email before the trip, Perala offered me transportation from the airport to my hotel. By bicycle of course. After consulting a map, I demurred, asking whether it was a good idea to try to make my way 20 kilometres into a strange city in a foreign country in the middle of winter in the middle of the night? "It's always a good time to ride a bike in Oulu," he replied with a little more enthusiasm than I would have liked. He promised to have a bike waiting for me at the airport. I swallowed hard and agreed.

I disembarked the plane into the clean, gleaming Oulu airport and one of the first things I noticed was something that struck me as quintessentially Nordic – near the front doors of the airport was an ice sculpture welcoming visitors, complete with a QR code carved into the ice that could be scanned by smart phones. It was high-tech and embracing of winter, all at once. I gathered my luggage and descended an escalator to await my fate.

I wheeled through the arrivals area and came upon two Finnish men with bicycles, one of whom held a sign with my name. I introduced myself, and they greeted me warmly. One took my suitcase, saying he would drive it back to the hotel in his car, then pushed a bike into my hands and was off. That left me with what I guessed would be my tour guide for the evening. A guide! This was great news. I wouldn't be wandering through suburban Oulu on my own in the middle of the night. That my guide was a stocky Finn with the long hair and the unruly chin puff of a Nordic death metal star bothered me not in the slightest. At least he knew the way to the city. To my surprise, he was dressed as a cyclist, in tights, a helmet and clip-in shoes, which contradicted what I had heard about European cyclists wearing everyday clothes when they ride a bike, but I quickly learned why: he had been escorting conference attendees from the airport all day. It was his 12th hour and hundredth kilometre on the bike that day. Yet, as he introduced himself, he seemed eager to hit the road again. "Hi, I'm Pekka," he said in accented English. "You ready?"

Off we pushed, Pekka on his cyclocross (which reminded me of home), me on my borrowed Kona, a sturdy commuter model with fenders and lights. I didn't have time to harbour worries about a winter ride at one a.m. in a strange city because before I knew it, we were off, into the dark and snow.

Although a small airport, I was surprised that a bike path made its way straight to the front door of Oulu International. This I had never seen before. "Of course," Pekka said to me as we glided onto the path. "How else are you going to ride a bike to the airport?" That was my first encounter with a trait that would crop up often during the next week; something I'll call Scandinavian practicality. When it came to cycling, questions that seem endlessly debated at home had already been settled here, and when I raised them, like I did in this instance, the answers hit me with a dose of obviousness. Of course Pekka was correct – without a bike route, how else were you going to ride a bike to the airport? Back home, the response to such questions tend to be long-winded semi-philosophical forays into questions about an airport bike path's viability, or its influence on motor vehicle traffic, or its impact on taxis. Here, I would soon learn, such questions seem simplified. Want people to ride bikes? Make it easy for them.

At a brisk clip, Pekka barrelled onto the pathway keeping up a running commentary about the unique history of Oulu as seen through municipal infrastructure. He was a recent graduate in urban planning, with much to say about bicycle infrastructure, with me, clad in jeans and fur-lined winter boots, pedalling hard to keep up. The path was cut in among the trees parallel to the highway as it made its way to the city of Oulu, along the shores of the Gulf of Kempele, a small bay in the Gulf of Bothnia, the northern arm of the Baltic Sea that separates Sweden to the west from Finland. The outside temperature was mild, despite it being the middle of the night, hovering around -6°c (21°F) with snow falling in lazy flakes brightened by the streetlights that dotted the pathway. Unlike the paths at home that were plowed down to the asphalt, this path was covered with packed snow, which I approached tentatively, thinking it slippery. "Did it just snow?" I asked Pekka. "Why hasn't this been plowed yet?" No, he shouted from up ahead, this is purposeful. City crews, he explained, always leave a layer of packed snow a few centimetres deep because it's easier to ride on, and keeps out the ice that can build up when the sun heats up the black asphalt. He demonstrated its safety by leaning into some dramatic turns and pulling hard on his brakes to a quick stop, which almost caused me to crash into the back of him. "Packed snow is great for bikes," he said. "Try it." Dutifully, but with less gusto, I mimicked his manoeuvres with nary a slip. He was right. Traction was strong and riding on it was sure. My first taste of the world's best winter bike city was impressive.

As we rounded our way towards Oulu, I was surprised by what I saw. It was quiet, with little traffic so late on a weeknight, but I didn't expect the areas we rode through to appear so suburban. After years of researching European bike culture, I expected dense, narrow cobblestone streets and old brick buildings, but the route from the airport ran alongside a highway that reminded me of home. We passed truck stops and big-box retailers. I counted five car dealerships. We rode past entrances to communities filled with single-family homes and wide front and back yards. It was the kind of environment you would never consider riding a bicycle through in North America because of the high speeds of vehicles on the road and narrow shoulders. The difference here, however, was the availability of an option. We didn't have to fight traffic on the highway because two metres away, separated by a buffer of land and a pile of plowed snow higher than our heads, was a wide, maintained, well-lit bicycle path.

As we rode, Pekka told me how a forward-thinking city planner back in the 1970s, when the city was transforming from a salmon and wood-tar generating northern outpost to a modern tech-friendly university city, saw the value in giving bicycles and feet priority in transportation. The city's first cycling plan was created in 1972, and two subsequent motivations helped push it along. The energy crisis of the 1970s hit small European economies hard, especially those with little domestic energy production. Unlike the vast offshore reserves of its newly wealthy neighbour Norway, Finland has almost no fossil fuel resources of its own, and relying on imports from Russia, its oil-rich giant neighbour to the east, especially after the fight for independence from the Soviet Union after the Second World War, was viewed warily by many Finns. The environmental movement that grew to prominence during the 1970s didn't skip Europe at this time and many Finns, newly urbanized after an agrarian past, felt strong connections to the outdoors and their forests. By the early 1980s, when a new downtown cycling plan was adopted by Oulu, city planners had discovered something about efficient and safe bicycle infrastructure. It worked. Oulu residents used bikes all the time.

As the city grew and new suburban communities were built, new pathways were constructed first. Today, there are 4.3 metres of bike infrastructure per resident in Oulu, a number they claim as the best in the world (In my own city, which often brags of its pathway network: 600 kilometres of pathways for one million residents equals 0.6 metres of pathways per resident). Over 40 years, the pathways in Oulu became a key part of transportation in the city used by residents, not because they were trying to be green or stay in shape or were motivated by ideology or politics, but because they offered the quickest and easiest way to get around. Cars are still the dominant form of transportation in Oulu, but Pekka assured me that the city's numbers were solid. The percentage of commuters cycling was 23 per cent, a good number if not the best in Europe (Amsterdam, for example, is nearing 40 per cent, while good North American cities hover around 2 per cent), but in Oulu, the number of people who ride through the winter was stellar. A third of cyclists keep it up year round, which is a huge number considering most cities don't even bother counting the number of cyclists in the winter because there are perceived to be too few.

Eventually, we came to the outskirts of the city and entered a residential community. The pathways crawled through a network of single-family homes with yards, often through back lanes. In spite of the

ungodly hour, the jet lag and the snow, I found myself enjoying the ride. The pathways made for an
easy outing, our pedalling kept me warm, and the
snow created an ethereal environment by muffling
the noise and reflecting orange from the street lights
above. Pekka turned out to be a lively tour guide,
seemingly unbothered by the late hour, whose ur-
ban-planning sensibilities wavered between pride in
the way his city had given bikes priorities and an-
noyance with the gaps in infrastructure, no matter
how minute. He scowled with impatience when a
bicycle traffic light took a full minute to turn green,
which amused me considering such lights don't even
exist in most North American cities. I bombarded
him with questions about bike infrastructure, and we
ended up taking the long way into the city, so he
could show me a series of bicycle underpasses beneath the highway that give cyclists unobstructed
routes, and the more leisurely parts of the pathway
that went through parks and forests. There was only
one thing missing from our tour, but I couldn't put
my finger on it until we entered the denser, more
urban part of the city downtown near my hotel.

This was more in keeping with my expectations
of a European city, even one as small and modern as
Oulu. Old brick buildings and narrower streets were

dotted with parked Fiats. Here, the pathways ran adjacent to roads, like wide sidewalks. Unlike sidewalks, however, there were round blue signs with icons of bikes and pedestrians, encouraging both groups to share the space. I rode with my head on a swivel, trying to take it all in. We passed the city square, which, unlike the rest of the streets, was free of snow. This was the famous heated square I had heard about months ago in Vancouver, a handful of cobblestoned city blocks in the shopping district that were as bare as summertime. We rode on, Pekka pointing out with disdain an underground parking garage that was under construction. "What's wrong with that?" I thought. Before I could get the question out, Pekka was already listing the ways he hated the idea, chief among them that it would encourage more people to take their cars downtown when he felt it was already congested. "What we need is more bike parking," he said. The complaints made me feel oddly comforted, knowing that, even here, the purported world's best winter cycling city, the debate about cars and bicycles was still raging.

As we passed a pair of teenagers kissing against the side of the building, he standing, she sitting on the seat of a parked bicycle, I realized what was missing in this tour: traffic. Other than a group of twenty-somethings pushing bikes from a night-club and obnoxiously laughing in the universal way of drunken university students, we saw nobody. The hour was too late. The city was sleeping. As we pulled into my hotel (Pekka seemed amazingly reluctant to end the tour despite passing the 100th kilometre of ferrying visiting delegates from the airport that day, and his schedule requiring him to be at the conference registering guests in only a few hours), I realized that without people, I wasn't seeing the real city. I had a top-notch tour of the ways bike infrastructure can be built into a city's core, but without seeing how people used it, I was missing something critical. It was like reading about music without hearing it. I needed to see the city at work. I thanked Pekka for getting me safely to the hotel. He surprised me with a hug. I checked into the boutique Hotel Lasaretti, and fell asleep quickly.

CHAPTER 13

In the early 2010s, similar arguments about urban development broke out in nearly every North American city, but those conversations tended to have a local flavour. As more people returned to cities from the suburbs, especially young people in search of more vibrant environments in the wake of the housing price implosion of 2008 and a decade of plummeting inner-city crime rates, they started demanding more efficient ways of getting around those traffic-clogged environments. Public transit was beefed up. Walking was re-recognized as an efficient way to get around after nearly 100 years of planning neglect. More people also started seeing the benefits of cycling. But as the popularity of urban cycling grew, the demands for infrastructure to accommodate it did as well, so cities went through public debates about the benefits and potential of cycling. No matter which city – from Montreal to Minneapolis to Portland to New York – the arguments against cycling were remarkably similar, and have almost always been proven wrong. "There aren't enough cyclists to justify bike lanes," is a familiar cry, when, in truth, the number of cyclists tends to grow as infrastructure is added. "Adding bike infrastructure will make vehicle congestion worse." The opposite usually happens. "Encouraging cycling will make streets more dangerous." Not only do separated bike lanes make it safer for cyclists, but most streets with bike lanes see significant reductions in car collisions too. There are virtually no downsides to encouraging cycling, if done properly.

What's different in each city, however, are uniquely local arguments, usually tied to the weather: in Arizona, it's claimed to be too hot to ride a bike in the summer; in Chicago, it's too windy; in Portland, it's too rainy; and, in northern cities, of course, it's too cold and snowy. The latter is a difficult argument to dispel. Our image of the perfect bike ride is on a sunny spring day with a gentle breeze and a young woman in a floppy hat riding with a French baguette in her basket. That perception tends to become reality in most cities. What usually happens when winter rolls in is that the number of cyclists tumbles, and those who do it are seen as zealots or oddballs.

So when I stumbled out the door of my hotel in

Oulu the next morning into weather that was hovering just below the freezing mark, with big flakes of snow falling, I needed to stop and stare. Those arguments about the unviability of winter cycling suddenly seemed irrelevant. A woman rode by on a bike; a twenty-something blonde in a knitted hat and fitted black coat, her basket filled with textbooks. Then came another young woman. Right behind her, I saw something I almost never see at home: an elderly lady on a bike, wearing waterproof snow pants and winter boots, pedalling nonchalantly through the falling snow. I stepped outside and gawked down the pathway in both directions. The route heading into downtown was criss-crossed with people on bikes laying fresh tracks in the snow. Most rode upright step-through bikes with baskets up front and carriers on the back, the kind of machine we'd refer to derisively back home as a granny bike, or, as I often hear about on my own cruiser, a girly bike. These bikes, however, were being powered by men in business suits, well-dressed young students and, yes, even grannies. In the darkness of the morning, all of the bikes had lights, most drawing power from hub dynamos, an attachment to the front wheel that draws power from the tire's movement. In the few moments I stood there, slightly agog at the number of people riding, I realized I had probably, in just a few minutes, seen more people riding in the snow than I ever had in my life. I was excited to see more, so I forced my dumbfounded mouth shut, keyed open the wheel lock on the hotel bike I borrowed, which had two inches of snow on the seat, and merged into the bike traffic streaming by.

The flow of bikes on the pathway was slower than I had got used to at home, but then again, I rarely encountered other cyclists at home to slow me down. Here, there was enough bike traffic to keep things at a brisk but manageable pace. As I found out the night before, the packed snow made for great footing on the ground, and the cyclists around me pedalled in confidence, with none of the tentative slips and wobbles that winter can bring up elsewhere. I moved past the steaming Oulu river, which was partly frozen over, and I followed the path through a park and into as lovely a winter scene as I had ever witnessed. Trees held shoulders of snow, while white wooden bridges took us over frozen streambeds, through quaint wooden archways and past small black lamp-posts. The falling snow softened everything, even though the people around me moved as purposefully as commuters should. I passed pedestrians walking forcefully with briefcases, and groups of seniors out for their morning constitutionals with Nordic walking poles in their hands.

I made my way out to the suburbs, where I saw plenty of cars on the roads, but I rarely encountered them because the pathways kept me separate. I was forced to cross intersections regularly, but there were several underpasses dug beneath the highways and busier roads. I passed a school just as children were gathering for the day, and unlike the schools back home that would have been clogged with legions of parents in sport-utility vehicles dropping kids off at this time of day, here the bike-racks were hosting most of the traffic. I was surprised to see kids that looked as young as six or seven riding their bikes independently to school, no helicopter parents hovering nearby to ensure their safety. This, I figured, was as much a product of the country's attitudes toward parenting and the community's small size as it was about road safety, but it made me wonder if we wouldn't see more kids riding their bikes unescorted to school if there was simply a safe way to get there.

As I rode on, the suburbs gave way to downtown Oulu, and the pathway changed. I found myself on the same urban routes as I had the night before, which really were glorified sidewalks; wider than usual, yes, but shared between cyclists and pedestrians. The difference now was that they were packed with commuters. At a junction, I stopped and pulled off to the side to observe the commuter ballet that played itself out on the pathways. Cyclists moved slower here, but still fast enough to gingerly overtake pedestrians. Those who were walking seemed aware of the bikes all around them, and instinctively stepped out of the way when necessary. At intersections, cars still had priority. Cyclists and pedestrians stopped to wait for the walk signal, but vehicle traffic moved slowly – there was usually one lane for cars in each direction – to accommodate the legions of bikes and pedestrians filling up every intersection.

As I explored the streets, something felt different from when I rode through downtown at home, and it took me a moment to figure out what it was. As I came to the downtown pedestrian area – the heated section demarcated by a solid line of snow where the underground warmth began – it struck me that the difference was in my gut. Getting around felt gentler somehow, like the tension of cycling downtown had eased, and the knot in my stomach that I didn't even realize I carried when I negotiated for space on roads with cars and trucks at home was gone. I could see immediately that Oulu's shared pathways weren't perfect; I saw at least one bicycle get a little too close to a passing walker. But the presence of so many bikes and the give-and-take on the shared routes between cyclists and pedestrians altered the tone of the downtown. It was quieter, slower and less stressful. My worries changed. At home, I tend to ride downtown with an anxiety-generated image in my head, that of my body being crushed under the wheels of a delivery truck while the driver chats on a cellphone. Here, the image I worried about was clipping a pedestrian with my handlebar, sending them spinning into the snow onto their butt. That's a serious concern not to be discounted, but the difference in those images was visceral. Riding in Oulu, with the concern about being killed nearly gone, I felt palpably safer. A lot of that can be attributed to the smaller size of the city. Oulu is about a tenth the size of Calgary, so there were obviously fewer people in a downtown that lacked the skyscrapers and commercial buzz I was accustomed to. The difference, however, seemed deeper than that. I felt welcome on a bike, rather than the sense that I was an invader.

A few blocks later, I stopped my bike again to observe. Back home, on my cycling blog, I had been habitually taking photographs of full bike racks whenever I encountered them as a cheeky way of providing evidence that cyclists were indeed out there, battling vehicles on the streets as an everyday mode of transportation. I'd capture a dozen bikes parked outside an office building downtown, or two dozen near the neighbourhood farmer's market on a warm summer afternoon. I would post these images to my blog, and cyclists would get so excited by them that I started labelling the photographs as bike-rack porn. It was a silly, throwaway habit that tended to disappear in winter because I could never find a full bike rack. Now that I came upon the bike rack outside of a department store in downtown Oulu, however, my photos seemed positively naive. Here, in the middle of February under snowy skies, was a rack overflowing with hundreds of bikes, so many that dozens were parked alongside secured with wheel locks because their riders weren't able to find a spot in the rack. It was a bird's-nest of tires, baskets and handlebars. I had never seen so many bikes in one spot, and it made my bike-rack porn back home feel like a quaint farm-girl's boudoir photo. As far as bike-rack porn went, this was Larry Flynt stuff: dirty, explicit and thrilling.

Later that night, I took another spin through the city. Darkness came early because of the northerly latitude, but that did little to stem the flow of bicycles. The after-work commute was lit by hundreds of bicycle headlights. I made my way toward the water-front, where a network of pedestrian/cyclist bridges spanned the delta of the Oulu River. I stood at a pathway junction beneath a directional sign, where nearby a huge pile of snow was being carved into a children's play area for the forthcoming weekend's winter festival, and watched a stream of bikes criss-cross their way through the city: students with books piled in their baskets; mothers pulling trailers loaded with toddlers; businessmen in suits with waterproof shells pulled over their pants. I joined the stream of commuters, but rode with less resolve. I tended to hold up the flow with my gawking. At a waterfront pub in an old brick building, dozens of bikes were parked out front as the sounds of laughter and music escaped whenever the door opened. At Hesburger, a Finnish fast-food burger chain, two teenagers wheeled up in the snow, one riding on the crossbar of a bike while the other pedalled. At the supermarket, two middle-aged women chatted as they loaded groceries into their baskets and rode off together. All of these scenes were thrilling to me in their nonchalance. Back home, riding in the winter was an atten-tion-grabber. Here, as I pedalled back to my hotel for the night, I realized what excited me was the sheer ordinariness of it all. Riding a bike in Oulu was as novel a decision as taking the bus or driving a car. But, as I was to learn the next day, the mundanity of winter cycling in Oulu is what made it so unique.

CHAPTER 14

I spent the next two days in Oulu holed up in the downtown Holiday Inn, eating the cheap pastries and lukewarm coffee that are de rigueur at conferences all over the world. To an outsider, this gathering wouldn't have seemed different than any other business conference anywhere: mostly middle-aged men wearing cheap suits or dress shirts without ties, and carrying briefcases and backpacks. As I spent time with this international group, however, I quickly picked up a sense of fraternity. There was a feeling of long-lost togetherness here, of having finally found each other. Most of these people had spent their lives riding bicycles in the snow in isolation. Their co-workers called them crazy, their friends had long rolled their eyes at their assertions that winter cycling was a good idea, and family members had stopped humouring their diatribes about the benefits society was missing out on because so few people bothered to ride in winter. Now, they were finally among friends. They had lived underground their whole lives and now, here they were, exposed and blinking in the sun together.

Over the two days, there were earnest presentations from Scandinavian traffic engineers about plowing and sanding. We heard from a Swedish researcher about the biggest safety risks of riding bicycles in the winter (surprisingly, most injuries came, not from collisions with cars or slipping on ice, but from old people hurting themselves getting on and off a bike. Somebody, please invent a bike that's easy for senior citizens to mount and dismount). We heard how difficult it is to find places in busy cities to dump snow that has been removed from streets and bike lanes. We heard the biggest problem for most cities in the winter isn't snow, cold or slush, but ice, and the best solution for that is something nobody likes: salt. It's bad for the environment, it corrodes bikes and cars, and it doesn't work in all temperatures, but dumping salt on ice does a better job increasing traction than anything else we currently use.

What struck me most out of the two-day conference, however, was how little we know about urban winter cycling. In many cities, especially those select European ones where cycling has been encouraged and accommodated for 30 years, the needs and behaviour of cyclists have been studied deeply, in the same way driving has been studied for 80 years, to better understand and plan for transportation infrastructure. In the great cycling cities of Europe, such as Amsterdam and Copenhagen, city planners know where cyclists are coming from, where they are going, when they ride and who they are. Even cities that put little more than lip-service into accommodating cyclists – which, until the early 2010s, included most cities in the world, even those in Europe – have a decent sense of how many people are pedalling to work because of yearly commuter counts. But almost all of that information is collected in the summer and winter is a data blackout. How many people ride in the winter? Why do they ride in the winter? What prevents them from riding? What could be done to encourage them? There were only a few studies that addressed these big questions. Now, at this conference, all these people excited about finding like-minded winter-bike devotees were starting to realize how little they knew, and how much work lay ahead.

That lack of information was exposed during the first presentation of the conference: a talk by Timo Perala, the conference organizer with the unruly beard who had invited me to attend. He had done more than anyone to pull these people together, and he was clearly buzzing in the early part of the conference. Youthful and energetic, but naturally reserved in that Finnish way, Perala was clearly invigorated with the response to his idea of gathering the world's experts on winter cycling, and on the first day he was hopping between welcoming guests and doing interviews for Finnish media, most of whom covered the conference as a bit of a novelty, a bunch of wacky cyclists not smart enough to put their bikes away for winter (outside of Oulu, winter cycling, even in Finland, was still rare). Prior to the start of the conference, Perala had spent months pulling together information from the scientific literature about winter cycling, and had the idea of kicking off the event by determining the top ten winter cycling cities in the world. It was a great idea because he knew it would get people talking and spark some nationalistic competitiveness among delegates, which is always a good way of getting things started. The problem, however, was that there were so few cities with enough good information about winter cycling to compare. He gamely pushed on.

Eventually, Perala came up with a formula to measure winter cycling in a city. He looked at four factors:

1. The length of bicycle paths available in each

city, measured proportionately as metres per resident.

2. The cycling modal split, which examined that old cyclist favourite of the percentage of commuters using bikes.
3. The percentage of people commuting to work on bicycles in the winter.
4. The final measure was the severity of winter measured by the length of the season and the number of snow days, meaning, basically, the more harsh the winter the higher the score.

You could debate his criteria – and many did – but it was a starting place.

What Perala found was nearly 100 cities with more than 50,000 inhabitants that exist in what might be called the world's northern "winter zone," in which considerations for winter cycling could, or should, be a factor in transportation planning. Most of those cities, however, collected almost no data about winter cycling, particularly in Russia and, what's even more interesting, China, where some colder cities have huge numbers of cyclists, even after 20 years of economic growth in which cycling has fallen from the primary mode of transportation to something stigmatized as an activity for the poor.

Where data did exist, however, Perala found some

fascinating stories. In North America, only three cities passed the threshold of having more than 5 per cent of commuters on bikes: Montreal, Minneapolis and Portland. Portland scored poorly on Perala's scorecard because of its mild winter. Montreal and Minneapolis have real winters, but fared less well because the number of year-round cyclists simply couldn't match some European cities, or there wasn't enough information about winter bicycling conditions.

The most compelling stories about winter cycling were in Europe. Interestingly, the great cycling centres of Amsterdam and Copenhagen didn't make Perala's list. Their winters were too mild for him; neither could quite muster enough cold and snow to equal the top contenders. After crunching all of his numbers, what Perala was left with was a list of ten small Nordic cities that, based on his criteria, were the most bike-friendly winter cities in the world:

1. Oulu, Finland
2. Linköping, Sweden
3. Uppsala, Sweden
4. Umeå, Sweden
5. Örebro, Sweden
6. Joensuu, Finland
7. Karlstad, Sweden

8. Rovaniemi, Finland
9. Jyväskylä, Finland
10. Luleå, Sweden

As Perala presented his list on a PowerPoint presentation during the first hour of the conference, I scanned the room to see the few faces of the other North Americans. They looked as confused as I did. Where were these places? I had never heard of them. As Perala talked, I plugged into Wikipedia on my computer, and realized there was a reason I hadn't heard of them. None had a population over 150,000 – Uppsala, Sweden, which houses the country's oldest university and is located about 70 kilometres north of Stockholm, was the biggest, with a population of 140,000. Perala's list, it seemed to me, was tailor-made to heap praise on the cities that were just like Oulu – blessed with small populations of active people who were scarce enough for cyclists and pedestrians to comfortably share infrastructure during winters that were snowy, predictable and relatively mild.

As I sat next to him later that day, I pushed Perala on this question a bit. He was a bit sheepish about his list, knowing that his criteria was pretty strict, but he also defended it by saying these cities had an advantage because data was available. He viewed his list as a starting point and was hoping more cities might see the value in collecting information about winter cycling. Perhaps future lists would be more comprehensive, he said.

While we were eating a Holiday Inn buffet lunch of smoked salmon, I asked Perala about Oulu. Why do the people here embrace cycling? Was there something genetic, or something cultural, that got people outdoors in the winter in such large numbers? Perala shrugged. "No," he said. "It's just easy to do." The pathway system, which had been built up over several generations, makes it fast and simple to get around on a bike, and city crews make sure the pathways are usable in winter, so that's why people get around on bicycles. I found this a little unsatisfying. It seemed too simple an explanation. "Come on," I said. "Finns must have some kind of natural affinity for winter that we North Americans have lost over the years." Reluctantly, Perala admitted to enjoying "four seasons," but said he had no particular love for winter. Riding a bike in Oulu in winter is just easy.

I left that conversation still feeling a little skeptical about the simplicity of Perala's explanation. Later that day, I was catching a bit of fresh air outside when another conference attendee emerged, and we got to talking. He wasn't a participant; rather, he worked for a software company and was at the conference to hawk a product built to connect conference delegates through social media. It turns out he was an expat: a tall, portly American with a thin beard and a chatty demeanour, named Jason. He was raised in the Midwest and had married a Finn he met in the U.S. He lived in Canada for a time before finally relocating to Oulu a couple of years ago. I asked him about bicycling in Oulu. If anybody would have insight into some uniquely Finnish cultural trait that predisposed Finns to the outdoors in winter, it would be an outsider living here.

He, however, wasn't all that interested in examining the Finnish psyche. Once I had expressed interest in cycling, there was something else he wanted to talk about. Excitedly, he pointed out his bike to me, which was lined up amid dozens parked outside the hotel lobby. Like a baby boomer showing off his restored Mustang, Jason gingerly pulled out his ride and showed it off. It was an army-green Helkama Jääkäri, a civilian version of the Finnish military bicycle famously used by soldiers to fight off the Nazis and the Soviets during the Second World War, when Finland's military developed a reputation for punching above its weight. The bike, made in Finland, was rugged and comfortable, with sturdy fenders and lights, a three-speed transmission and an upright riding style. It wasn't flashy, but was the kind of sturdy machine that could be ridden for a lifetime and then be bequeathed to grandchildren. In a city in which even the men rode step-through bikes that would be sniggered at home as granny bikes, this bike oozed machismo – "It helped fight off the Red Army!" Jason said. "I love my bike."

I expressed a little surprise at seeing an American, raised to fetishize cars, crowing over a measly bicycle. Jason didn't deny the irony. "When we first moved here we had a car," Jason told me. "But it's just easier to get around here on a bike, so we sold the car after a while." No, he hadn't yet learned to enjoy winter. No, he didn't consider himself a cyclist. He simply liked the convenience that came with getting around on a bike, and it was a hell of a lot less expensive than owning a car, he said. After the bike became his primary mode of transportation, he invested some money in his Helkama and came to love it. I noticed something else: Jason didn't say so, but I think he liked the bike because its history in the military made him feel a little more Finnish. As the snow fell outside the hotel, I took a photo of Jason and his Helkama, the American with a smile of pride over a Finnish bicycle, and I realized there was something cultural about this situation that lent some insight into my central question about winter cycling, but not in the way I originally thought. Sure, Finns are more active and outdoorsy than typical North Americans, but they aren't born to love bicycles or winter. I chatted with conference delegates from the capital city of Helsinki, for example, who expressed frustration with riding a bike in that city, especially in winter, because of the lack of bicycle infrastructure (the number of bicycle commuters in Helsinki is only slightly higher than most North American cities). So it wasn't an inherent Finnish trait that lent itself to winter cycling. What Jason showed me was that it was the other way around: the convenience of the bike, and a city that accommodated it, had given him a way into a year-round bicycle culture.

CHAPTER 15

On my way home from Finland, I decided to make another European stop. Oulu had given me new insight, but my big question about whether winter cycling was viable everywhere was still nagging me. Oulu had been a different world, but I couldn't help thinking that it was almost too different, too perfect. The weather, the winter conditions, the pathway network, the population and demographics – all of it seemed perfectly suited to accommodate winter cycling. Many of these conditions simply didn't exist in other cities. What I needed was more perspective.

Some old friends from Calgary were living in Copenhagen, and they graciously offered me a room for a couple of days, so off I went. Copenhagen, I thought, would offer me another point of view. Over the past 30 years, Copenhagen had evolved from a typical car-clogged metropolis to one of the world's greatest bike cities. For anybody who cared about urban cycling, it had become a living example of what a city can do when politicians and civic leaders decide to accommodate bikes. And, just as importantly for my mission, the city experienced winter (a much different winter than Oulu, but a winter nonetheless). I needed to see how other bike-friendly cities dealt with the season everybody seems to hate.

A flight from Oulu to Helsinki, followed by a hop over the Baltic Sea and the southern tip of Sweden and I arrived at the Copenhagen airport. Within minutes, I was riding the metro into the city, which, not incidentally, was suitably efficient for a country with a reputation for design and economy. I climbed the stairs from the underground stop in the city and when I reached the surface I almost fell over from shock. If the full bike rack that blew me away in Oulu was Larry Flynt bike-porn, I had just stumbled into a Roman orgy. The sheer number of bikes parked at this Copenhagen metro station left me agog. There were thousands of bicycles all crammed together, all secured by wheel locks. Nearly a full block was overflowing with bicycles of every stripe: Dutch cargo bikes, upright pedal bikes, rusty mountain bikes and aging granny bikes. On my first step into the city, I saw more bikes in one place than I had ever witnessed. This, I thought, was going to be good.

I managed to pull my eyes away because I had arranged a meeting and was running late. I hoofed it a few blocks across Islands Brygge, a harbourfront area reclaimed from the sea in the 1800s and converted into an industrial area that had, by the 1950s, become a rough-and-tumble part of the city, famed for producing the brother-and-sister duo of Mikkel and Linse Kessler: he a professional boxer, she a trashy siliconed reality-TV star known for lugging around "Denmark's largest breasts." Although huge redevelopments since 2000 had turned the district into a fashionable residential area, it maintained a seedier side. Under the grey skies of a Denmark winter, with a thin soggy layer of snowfall that was melting away from all but the coolest nooks of the city, I walked on.

Even here, the impact of Copenhagen's famous cycle tracks could be seen. Not on every street, but on strategically located thoroughfares, bikes enjoyed separation from both motor vehicles and pedestrians. These cycle tracks, which are basically a third portion of transportation infrastructure separate from sidewalks and the road, give bikes a safe, efficient place to travel. On slower roads, they abut the streets and sidewalk, but alongside roads on which cars travel faster, and the danger for cyclists is greater, there is a buffer: either a strip of grass or a row of parked cars. On these roads, the separation is important. Moving from the outside in, it looks like this: a sidewalk for pedestrians, small buffer, cycle track, small buffer, parked cars, small buffer, road for cars. The same pattern is repeated on the other side of the road for traffic moving in the opposite direction. After being in the city only minutes, and on foot, the difference this made for cyclists was obvious. Bikes travelled everywhere, riders pushing on confidently and quickly, seemingly without the usual worries of being crushed by a vehicle.

I didn't, however, have much time to study. I had found my destination: one of the hundreds of lookalike brick multi-storey buildings that covered the blocks of Islands Brygge housed the city's bicycle traffic planners. I had arranged a meeting with Andreas Rohl, Copenhagen's bicycle program manager, whom I had first met back in Canada earlier that year. Back then, he was on leave from his job in Denmark, working for a year with a planning consultancy in Vancouver. He gave a talk about urban cycling in Calgary, and I was asked to introduce him. Tall, lean and bald, Rohl had a devilish smile and seemed to be endlessly surprised by his rock-star status among Canadian bicycle advocates, who viewed him with a kind of wistful longing for what he had helped build in Copenhagen. From his talk in Calgary, I could see why. In a city in which the automobile had almost completely taken over transportation in the 1960s, the popularity of the bike in Copenhagen by the 2010 bicycle census was breathtaking: 35 per cent of residents rode a bicycle to work or school every day. Sixty-eight per cent of Copenhagen residents rode a bike at least once a week. The city had built 350 kilometres of cycle tracks, 23 kilometres of on-street cycle lanes and 43 kilometres of other cycle routes that were painted green for identification. More than 1.2 million kilometres are travelled by bicycle in the city every day. When I first met him in Canada, Rohl was a little sheepish about those figures, not wanting to embarrass his hosts. In his time away from Denmark, he gave similar talks around North America, recounting Copenhagen's move towards the bicycle as a way of unclogging streets, improving the mobility of the populace and saving money – for cash-strapped cities, cycle tracks came at a fraction of the cost of roads and metro lines. Rohl also talked about the side benefits of enabling so much cycling, which include a quieter city, healthier people with reduced health care expenditures, reduced greenhouse gas emissions and more lively streets. In front of an already convinced audience back in Calgary, Rohl was treated like a prophet.

Now, back on his home turf, Rohl was back to being a bureaucrat, albeit a powerful and smiling one. He buzzed me into his office building, a rather bland and aging series of doors, and greeted me warmly. He offered to buy me lunch at the municipal cafeteria up on the fifth floor, and we sat down with our food trays over a Danish comfort meal of potatoes, beets and egg. Rohl had been back in Copenhagen for a few months, but seemed happy to see a Canadian face. He said he had enjoyed his time in Canada, and when I suggested he might have taught more about urban cycling than he learned, he gave a polite, only half-hearted protest. Working in North America for a year, he said, had given him a new perspective on cycling. For one thing, he continued, he never got used to the idea of bicycle commuting as exercise. Most Danes ride short distances on slower upright bikes, so sweat isn't a problem. They don't even bother wearing anything other than their regular clothes. Exercise to them, he said, is going for a jog after riding home from work. He also struggled with the problem of "dooring" in North America, in which cyclists are, not infrequently, injured when crashing into the opening door of a parked car. He says it took him some time to realize why this seemed to be a North American problem, but eventually attributed it to Danes having simply grown accustomed to checking their mirrors for cyclists before exiting the car, because bikes were always around. I thought separated cycle tracks built on the opposite side of the car might have something to do with it as well, but I didn't mention this to Rohl.

I asked Rohl about how he could be envied by bicycle planners in North America, considering the battle was mostly won in Copenhagen – he must be free of the endless debates about whether bikes belong on roads, or whether more cyclists is a good thing. He laughed. "Not so much," he said. While most Copenhagen residents seem to acknowledge that bikes have helped the city's population grow in a more efficient way, and recognize the benefits of cycling, the debates have yet to go away. In fact, his job might even be tougher now than in the early days of bicycle planning because the easy work was done. With a robust network of cycle tracks in place, his team struggled now to find space for more paths to meet demand. There were still many connections between bike lanes that needed to be completed. Those broken links had yet to be built because they were passed over as too difficult the first time around. "They are getting harder and harder to fill," he said.

Even here, in the city known as one of the most

bicycle-friendly cities in the world, there were other challenges still to be faced. Rohl said his group was working on revamping some of the first-generation cycle tracks because they were now too narrow. Their popularity, an increasing number of children on bikes, and the growing use of cargo bikes, meant more space was needed, but finding room in the constricted confines of an old European capital was tough (he laughed when I told him many people think there's not enough space for bike infrastructure on North American roads). The city also struggled with the popularity of cycling, particularly because of the demand for more bicycle parking. With entire blocks of city streets given over to bike parking overflowing with more and more bikes, Rohl said finding space was nearly impossible in some parts of the city. The increased use of cargo bikes, especially among young Danish families, made the parking problem even worse. Parking, he said, was what kept him up at night.

With a little prodding, Rohl took a moment to politely complain about the Copenhagen police, who wield political power in the country and remain opposed to some simple measures he thought might help make the city more bicycle-friendly still. Unlike Oulu, the great success of Copenhagen cycling is often attributed to the separation between motorists, pedestrians and cyclists. Each group has its own designated space, and that keeps movement safe and efficient for everyone. Rohl, however, thought there were some quieter areas of the city in which shared infrastructure would work. "We believe in planning for reality, not for the way we want people to behave," he said. The police, however, continued to nix such ideas because they worried about conflicts between groups. Rohl thought the police were being a little stubborn because they didn't want to have to sort out responsibility if there was a collision.

Still, some of Copenhagen's bicycle planners had moved onto new challenges. The city had just opened its first cycling "superhighway" in conjunction with neighbouring municipalities. These superhighways, which are basically bike paths that stretch deep into the surrounding suburbs and offer largely uninterrupted routes into the city complete with air pumps, foot rests at intersections, and the promise of a wave of green lights if cyclists travel at the speed limit, are intended to reduce the number of cars coming into the city from the populous 'burbs. Most bicycle trips in Copenhagen take place over short distances in the more urban parts of the city – there's a sense here, and earlier in Oulu, that anything further than about five kilometres was too far to expect people to ride a bike. This superhighway was the first attempt to stretch that distance and it runs along both sides of a busy freeway, where it was being monitored closely. It was billed as the next step in the city's bike-friend-liness, a way to further reduce car traffic and carbon emissions (although Rohl was loath to mention the environment when discussing bikes, saying reducing pollution is almost never a reason people choose to use a bike) by making it fast and easy for suburban-ites to ride a bike into the city. Indeed, within days of the superhighway opening, videos were posted on YouTube showing waves of smiling cyclists coasting alongside lines of cars stopped in traffic jams on the freeway. The success of the superhighway had yet to be determined, because it was so new, but Rohl said plans were being developed for hundreds of kilome-tres of such pathways, creating a network of routes stretching far into the surrounding communities. It struck me that, for many North American cities that lack the urban density of older European ones, this may be the most applicable part of Copenhagen's network of bike infrastructure, and would be well worth keeping an eye on.

All was not perfect in Copenhagen. Rohl did express a little envy toward Amsterdam, which is generally considered the most bike-friendly city in the world. The number of cyclists in the Dutch city was higher than in Copenhagen, and cycling was more a part of Dutch culture, Rohl thought. Mostly, however, he longingly eyed the factors that made it difficult to drive a car in Amsterdam – sky-high parking rates, horrible congestion, narrow, clogged streets. Although neither city had managed to implement a congestion fee like the one in place in London, in which vehicles entering the downtown area at certain times of day are charged a fee, Rohl said putting restrictions on vehicle use was the logical next step for cities hoping to improve urban mobility. Such decisions, however, are invariably political and even in the most bike-friendly municipalities in the world, no politician had yet mustered the will to have these restrictions implemented.

Then I broached the topic of winter. It was the middle of February, with snow on the ground, so I pulled out the statistics from the Copenhagen tourist office that I looked up before I travelled to the city. February in Copenhagen isn't sub-Arctic, but it isn't exactly balmy either. Daytime average temperatures hover around the freezing point for the month, and there is an average of 30 millimetres of precipitation. Numbers, however, only go so far in telling the story of winter in a city. Most of the precipitation in the winter months comes in the form of wet snow, which falls regularly if not in huge dumps. Much of a typical snowfall melts as it hits the warmer concrete, but it does accumulate often enough. Normally, it melts away within a few hours, but there are storms that blanket the city occasionally. Compared to more northerly cities, the winter weather is bearable, but the sogginess makes it tough to deal with. The wind can get cold, and when you're wet, that's no fun.

Rohl seemed a little surprised by my interest in the season. He didn't see it as a huge obstacle for cyclists. He was quick to point out that 80 per cent of people riding bikes in Copenhagen do it through the winter. Compared to back home, where the number of cyclists drops from 2 per cent of commuters down to practically zero, that's a huge figure.

When we finished our lunch and walked back towards Rohl's office, he offered to show me something. A few doors down from his, he knocked quietly and we entered a room a little larger than the average office filled with several computer monitors displaying slowly and constantly adjusting line graphs. A series of flip-through laminated maps hung from the wall next to a big monitor displaying six webcam videos of streets around the city. This, Rohl explained, was the hub of winter cycling in Copenhagen. Rohl invited a colleague named Jan Elvekjaer in to explain things. This was the spot where Elvekjaer and a coworker were tasked with monitoring winter conditions around the city. When the snow falls, they are glued to the screens, watching the webcam videos of busy cyclist spots around the city. "We love to see black roads without ice," Elvekjaer said. Ice, it turns out, is a big worry for winter cyclists, at least for those who work in this office. With such wet snowfall, if the temperature dips, ice can form quickly and starts to take its toll on those narrow road tires that most Copenhageners ride around on all year long.

Elvekjaer explained the monitors to me. The screens were connected to remote sensors. There were ten of them strategically buried all over the city, keeping a digital eye out for ice. The sensors measured a number of factors that can create ice on the cycle tracks: the amount of precipitation that has fallen, overall moisture, the temperature, and the makeup of the sky, whether clear or cloudy. Each measure was represented by a line graph on the screen that was constantly creeping to the right. If the lines crossed, the factors existed for the formation of ice and it would be time to hit the button. The button sends the city's fleet of salt trucks into action, spreading a melting agent over bike lanes and cycle tracks wherever it's needed. The button is pushed only a few times through the winter, Elvekjaer said, but he hedged a bit. I got the sense he was not telling me something. "We have to be careful when we push the button," he said. "It's expensive to send out the trucks." Not only is it expensive to salt a city, salt isn't exactly a crowd pleaser either. Back in Oulu, salt was a hot topic of debate. Salt isn't used everywhere. If the climate is too cold, salt is useless – its effectiveness stops at about –10°c (14°f). Some northern cities, like Oulu, don't require salt because the temperature rarely rises above freezing in the winter, meaning there is little meltwater to freeze. In more temperate climates, however, salt is a reluctant necessity for safe roads. It melts ice and adds traction in slippery areas, but it also corrodes vehicles, rusts bicycles, and is bad for waterways when washed off the streets. Here in environmentally conscious Europe, things must get pretty bad before the salt button is pushed, hence the trepidation in Elvekjaer's voice.

I nosed around Copenhagen's hub of winter cycling a bit more, but there wasn't much else to see. It certainly didn't run the risk of being confused with a NASA ground station. With fluorescent lighting and limp floor plants, this place looked, despite its lofty title, a little boring. In one of the most bicycle-friendly cities in the world, this seemed like a pretty minor accommodation for winter. Rohl said that other than plowing after big snowfalls – like Oulu, bike lanes are plowed before roads – the city of Copenhagen doesn't do anything else to accommodate cyclists in winter. That's it? More than 80 per cent of people in the city ride their bikes year round, with nothing more than some plows and some occasional salt. So how do people deal with winter?

Rohl shrugged his shoulders over this question. Having just returned from Canada, with its cold winter and virtually non-existent winter cycling, he understood my desire for a deeper answer. I was looking for a silver bullet. I wanted to hear about some measure that could apply at home to change things completely; so that winter cycling isn't viewed as something for zealots and the deranged, but a viable option for reasonable people. But there is no such measure. What about the cold and wet? The reasons people ride bikes in the winter, he said, are the same reasons they ride bikes in the summer – doing so is quick and convenient. You just have to dress for it.

I thanked Rohl for his time, but left his office feeling a little unsatisfied. I come from a country that is said to define itself by its winter. Winter is an ever-present goblin lurking over our shoulders all year round, and to just shrug it off as something that can beaten by dressing differently struck me as a blissfully naive perspective from somebody living in an enviously temperate climate. As for his time in Canada, Rohl spent most of it in Vancouver, the city with winters so mild the rest of Canada mocks it as being inhabited by creampuffs.

What I needed, I decided, was the perspective of somebody who understood what real winter is all about. Fortunately, I knew just the guy.

CHAPTER 16

On a wet Copenhagen morning in 2006, Mikael Colville-Andersen, an expat Canadian living in the city his mother grew up in, was riding a bicycle through the streets with his camera. Since relocating to the city after years of travelling, he was trying to make a living as a photographer and filmmaker. On this November day, he was on his way to work, doing some street photography, simply capturing some of the beautiful people making their way through the city. On one of those drab Scandinavian days with grey clouds and soft light that photographers adore, he was taking photos of the cyclists around him, capturing a series of people pedalling ahead of him, juxtaposed against the city's century-old brick buildings and the solid blue paint of the bike lanes beneath them. Waiting on a red light on Åboulevard in Frederiksberg, a borough of the city, a woman on a bike directly ahead of him caught Colville-Andersen's eye. As the traffic light changed, at a moment "when the muscles tense and the legs propel the bike forward," he snapped a photograph.

The image he caught was remarkable in a couple of ways. For one, it's a beautiful photograph, with perfect composition. He captured a striking image of a woman on a bike: blonde, slim and well dressed, the very picture of autumn Danishness in a long black coat and knee-high boots that disappear beneath her skirt. Secured to the rear carrier of her bicycle is her handbag, a splash of red that draws your eye. The streets are wet, and other cyclists criss-cross around her, streaming by in saturated colours that give the image an aura of timelessness. Because we can't see the woman's face, there's also a mystery and romance to the photograph that, for many viewers, gives rise to a simple question: how can someone ride a bike while looking so damn chic? What's even more remarkable about the photograph, however, is what happened next.

On one of his first days in Copenhagen, Colville-Andersen was staying with friends and needed to run some errands. Just take the bike parked out front, his friend offered. Outside the building, he came across a bike that looked like thousands of others across the city. He doesn't remember the bike specifically, but it was most likely plain and black, with an easy step-through frame that kept the rider upright. It had a carrier of some kind, either a basket up front or a rack on the back, and likely sported a little rust. It probably wasn't chained to a rack or tree, rather had a simple wheel lock that, when engaged, prevented the back tire from turning. He took the bike for some quick errands and returned, smitten with the experience.

The longer he lived in Copenhagen, the more interested in the bicycle he became. After being reared in North America, this was a profound difference in transportation and city life. Colville-Andersen was raised in my home city, Calgary, in a leafy older suburb that, by the time he was living there, was being overlooked by many young homebuyers in favour of newer, more far-flung developments that boasted bigger houses and quiet cul-de-sacs. Colville-Andersen says he never considered himself a cyclist, but remembers tooling around his burgh as a child, like millions of other kids of the 1970s, exploring the neighbourhood, getting into minor trouble, and going home when he got hungry. As he grew into his teenage years, his family moved around a bit – he even spent some time in Alberta's oil sands capital of Fort McMurray – and he followed the pattern of most North Americans and left the bicycle behind. But after some travel and a decision to settle in Copenhagen, where he married, had two children and then divorced, the bicycle re-entered his life. Colville-Andersen was fascinated with the way Danes in the city used the bike as a practical form of transportation. Nobody considered themself a cyclist. Nobody wore cyclist clothing and few of them even wore helmets. Bikes were practical and efficient, and that was the end of it for most people. But Colville-Andersen noticed the way bicycles gave life to city streets. In the already fashionable European capital, he liked how bicycles added a certain style to the people on them. There was a kind of symbiosis between cycling and fashion – because nobody changed the way they dressed to ride a bike, their natural style came through on the streets.

His camera started working overtime. After capturing that image of the girl on the bike with her red handbag while on his way to work that day, Colville-Andersen posted it to the Internet. The response was immediate and gratifying. "Great photo – the washed-out sky, the guy leaning into the curve, and of course the yummy girl with the long skirt on the bike really make it," wrote one commenter about the photo. Another was less subtle: "Super duper holy moly rock steady head banging great photo!"

Encouraged, Colville-Andersen started taking and posting more photos of fashionable Copenhageners on bikes. The idea evolved into a blog. He named it Copenhagen Cycle Chic, with the meaning of the word "chic" a little different to Danes than North Americans, a kind of well-put-together sophistication rather than a high-fashion snootiness.

Over the next couple of years, the blog became a veritable phenomenon. It drew viewers from all over the world interested, on one level, in looking at beautiful people, but also interested in a different kind of cycling. The blog began at a time when interest in urban cycling was on an upswing, and Colville-Andersen's Cycle Chic not only caught that wave, but also propelled it. He gave the movement a defining image, and an aspirational one at that. It was cycling culture writ in beauty, and it was inspiring. Cyclists in other cities started riding Copenhagen style, dressing "for the destination, not the journey," as Colville-Anderson likes to say. Soon, bloggers in other cities started emailing Colville-Andersen asking for his blessing to set up cycle chic blogs where they lived. Soon there were Amsterdam Cycle Chic and Paris Cycle Chic blogs. Mainstream news outlets started writing about this Danish blogger who was inspiring a heretofore unheard-of cycling and style movement. *The Guardian* described Colville-Andersen as "The Sartorialist on two wheels," after the famous New York fashion blogger. Another writer described Colville-Andersen's original Cycle Chic image as "the photo that launched a million bicycles." Today, there are dozens of Cycle Chic chapters from Rio de Janeiro to Brighton to Boulder, Colorado. Even Colville-Andersen's childhood city of Calgary has one.

Colville-Andersen, meanwhile, noticed that what fascinated people about his blog wasn't so much the fashion, but the way people rode bikes in Copenhagen. There was some pent-up interest in creating more bicycle-friendly cities, and, as the guy who had given urban cycling a look, he spotted an opportunity for something bigger. He started examining not just the people who ride bikes, but the way they ride them. He studied their attitudes. He got to know Copenhagen's bicycle planners, like Andreas Rohl, and examined what kind of bike infrastructure worked and what didn't. He looked at what other cities were doing to accommodate bikes or, perhaps just as useful, what other cities were doing to discourage cycling. His persona developed from fashionista to urban cycling guru. He became the country's go-to third-party expert on cycling, beloved by the media, especially the foreign press, as a spokesperson who could explain why cyclists in their countries were all talking about Copenhagen. It didn't hurt that he was good-looking and great with a sound bite, unafraid to mock conventions and chide government inaction everywhere. Soon, you could see him everywhere, from bits on cycling on Al-Jazeera to a TED talk, in which he gave a provocative speech convincingly arguing why you shouldn't wear a helmet while cycling.

To capture all of this, Colville-Andersen launched his own consultancy, named Copenhagenize. On his website, he details the city's bicycle-friendly initiatives with the same mix of irreverence and common sense that made him a media darling. Five years after its launch, Copenhagenize is a firm with a handful of employees that offers consultation for bicycle planning bureaucrats, while designing and building infrastructure projects all over the world.

This was the guy who buzzed me into his flat in Frederiksberg on that February day, graciously offering me a glass of wine to chase the chill out of my bones. He was keen to talk about winter, as my earlier email suggested, but when he found out I had just attended the winter cycling conference in Oulu, he was full of questions for me. He knew of the city, and was aware of its reputation for winter cycling, but had yet to visit. "What are the paths like?" "How's the snow clearing?" "How many people were at the conference?" "How many North Americans were at the conference?" Satisfied, he leaned back and put another question to me: "So, you're interested in winter cycling?"

Over the next couple of hours, Colville-Andersen laid out an approach to winter cycling in Copenhagen that was much different in philosophy, but surprisingly similar in practicality, to Oulu.

The biggest difference that struck me was one of attitude. Residents of Oulu seemed almost proud of the harshness of their winter. I heard more than one Finnish cycling advocate dismiss the winters of more southern cities as a mere inconvenience compared to theirs. "That's not winter," they'd say. "Not real winter, like ours." What Colville-Anderson presented, however, was a more businesslike, practical attitude toward the season. Like Rohl earlier that day, Colville-Andersen saw winter not so much as an impenetrable force of nature, but an obstacle to be overcome, and not a particularly difficult one at that. He praised the city's snow clearing, which prioritized bike lanes and cycle tracks over roads. He also said Copenhagen residents were pretty good about clearing snow from their own sidewalks. He thinks ice is a problem, but a minor one – he says he rarely hears of people injured in bicycle crashes related to weather. "We just deal with it," Colville-Andersen said. "We've kind of cancelled winter."

Colville-Andersen was a little curious about why I thought winter was such an obstacle to cycling. I told him I thought he was downplaying the discouraging effects of winter, just like Rohl had. After all, I pointed out, statistics from Rohl showed that 20 per cent of Copenhagen cyclists give up their bikes in the winter. He replied, "I often turn that around and say 80 per cent keep riding year round – only 20 per cent stop. That's still a great number. I think it's fair enough. If people don't want to do it in the winter, I understand. We'd rather see them riding for all the health benefits, but you can always take public transit." And those same statistics from Rohl pointed out that Colville-Andersen was right. The number of users of Copenhagen's first-rate transit system go up in the winter.

The biggest accommodation most Danes make for winter cycling, he said, was simply to dress for it and wear warmer clothes. Not cycling clothes, just dressing the way you would if you had to walk to work in the winter.

I smiled at this suggestion, considering it echoed

almost exactly what Rohl and people in Oulu told me, but inside I was feeling frustrated. Just dress for it? That's it? After all I had gone through in my quest to find out whether winter cycling is a viable option, the solution is to wear a scarf? It still seemed too simple a solution. So I pushed Colville-Andersen on the issue. He was in a unique position to understand both the practical and the cultural differences between Copenhagen and North American cities, and especially my home city. Sure, Copenhagen's winter is milder than some, but as I learned that day, it still gets uncomfortably cold and snowy. So why does just the threat of winter send most North American cyclists scurrying back into their cars, leaving only the hard-core cyclists to ride through the winter, to be greeted like freaks and zealots when they arrive at work, while most Copenhageners seem to deal with winter by simply putting on a pair of boots and mittens? "The main problem in North America is that cycling is seen as an extreme sport," he said. "It's really hard to break that mould."

In some ways, Colville-Andersen has spent years trying to create a new image. The civic vision he espouses seems both seasonally and geographically agnostic. Want more cyclists in a city?

Colville-Andersen's solution is to make cycling the quickest route from A to B. Remove the idea that cycling is a subculture. Make it practical for everybody, including children, grandparents, mothers with toddlers and jocks. Turn the bike from an exercise machine to a household appliance; Colville-Andersen is often comparing it to a vacuum cleaner. If all that is in place, he says, winter will cease being an obstacle. "People here just adjust for winter," he said. "They just do it."

CHAPTER 17

I stayed for a couple of nights in Copenhagen with friends I had known for years back in Calgary who had moved to Denmark a couple of years previously, when Clint, a strapping former university football player, took a job teaching economics at a Danish university. Along with his Canadian wife Melanie and their two young children, the family moved to Copenhagen, found a home in the suburbs and set about becoming as Danish as they could, which included giving up their dream of buying a car, because of the costs, which seemed astronomical to them (they had not yet adopted the slight guilt-induced embarrassment at yearning for a car the way most Danes do). Onto bicycles this expat family went, and by the time I visited, they had pretty much adjusted to a car-free life. Clint rode more than ten kilometres to work every day. Melanie had become a master at navigating the Copenhagen public transit system. The kids walked to school, and had even managed to keep a little Canadianness by signing up for the local hockey team, which required them to lug their hockey bags on their backs when they rode bikes to the rink.

After a hearty breakfast, Melanie sent me off on her candy-apple red Jupiter upright bike to explore the city like a real Copenhagen resident. If ever there was a time to act on the old "when in Rome" mantra, this was it, so I decided to dress the part. That meant not dressing for the journey like a cyclist, but for my destination, as an off-season bike tourist. I left my tight waterproof pants in my suitcase, pulled on a pair of jeans and, mindful of Colville-Andersen's assessment of Danes who dress for the weather, stuffed the pockets of my winter jacket with backup scarves, mittens and a warm hat. I refused Melanie's offer of a helmet, because that's what a Dane would do, but happily accepted the sandwich she had made for me ("Don't buy that overpriced tourist food," she wisely advised), and the GPS unit she dropped into the basket of the bike, just in case I got lost. She waved goodbye while the kids gleefully threw snowballs at me in retaliation for the ones I lobbed their way earlier and I was off.

I felt a little self-conscious at first, riding a woman's bike, a red one no less, that was too small, until I pulled onto a road behind another dude riding an identical bike. Danes may be effortlessly fashionable in their clothing choices, but their bicycle choices rarely seem motivated by style. Within only a few blocks, I came upon my first Copenhagen cycle track. Out here in the suburbs on a Saturday, the traffic was relatively light, but riding on the cycle track already felt different than a winter ride at home. Snow had accumulated in the shadows of the curb, which reduced the amount of riding space I had, and I occasionally breezed over a patch of ice, but being separated from traffic in this way made me feel safe. Riding this style of bike felt different too. My cruiser bike at home often felt slow and dorky, but here everyone rode upright, and the style made me feel more relaxed. I hadn't realized it, but back home I had grown accustomed to fighting for my space on the roads, something I always attributed to a lack of bike infrastructure, but now I started thinking it was also a result of my choice of bike. On my commute, I was always hunched over, always pushing myself to go faster, to generate some sweat as part of my daily workout – that's part of the reason I like riding a bike – but here, it was different. The battle for space on the road was gone, and sitting upright, I felt a little more comfortable.

As I neared the city, the cycle track took me the

entire way alongside but separated from the road. I started to realize how fundamentally the bicycle had become a part of the city. I was shocked at the number of small, locally owned bicycle shops I rode past. Back home, there were only a handful to support a million residents in my city. But here, there seemed to be one on every block. I stopped counting when I got past 20, and that was within the first hour of my day. On billboards and advertisements, the bicycle was given a prominent place. The image of the bike was shorthand for the city, a quick and easy way for advertisers to announce themselves as someone who belongs. The bike was given prominence at metro stops and in front of cafes and shopping areas. I never got used to seeing the thousands of bikes parked everywhere; even complete roads were given over to bike parking.

As I rode the bike into downtown Copenhagen, it took a little while for me to adapt to the rhythms of the city. Eventually I learned to trust the infrastructure. I watched the traffic lights built for bikes, and they safely got me through busy intersections. In other cities, cyclists often complain that bike infrastructure vanishes just when you need it – traffic planners often cut off bike lanes before busy intersections because they don't want to be liable for cyclists injured in those busy areas, which means cyclists can't trust the lanes. That didn't happen to me in Copenhagen. The bike infrastructure was in place almost everywhere I needed it. When I came upon one intersection that required a left turn, I worried about how I might execute it. I didn't want to cross traffic, bike or car, so I hesitated. But as I came closer, I saw a little jut out to the right that took me out of the way of traffic, spun me in the right direction, and after a bike traffic light turned green, enabled me to, rather boringly, complete my left turn without incident. That was my first experience with the famous Copenhagen left.

I even had my own cycle chic moment. Despite wearing "everyday" clothes on this ride, I quickly realized I was badly underdressed by Copenhagen standards. Blue jeans? Puffy ski jacket? What was I thinking? At one moment, I was surrounded by a half dozen beautiful women on bikes, all well-dressed in heels, long black coats and scarves flying behind them in the wind. While I tried to enjoy the moment without feeling self-conscious about my Costco shoes, the second part of the cycle chic mantra struck me. Cycle chic isn't about just looking good, according to Colville-Andersen, it's adapting the bike to your everyday life. These women were a test case in how to do that. While I wobbled in the middle of the group, trying to keep my line straight, one woman, in heels and a skirt, a handbag in her basket, chatting on the phone through hands-free earbuds with a cigarette pursed between her lips, signalled and executed a perfect left-hand turn without missing a beat. I had a lot to learn.

More deeply, however, I instinctively felt like I was in control of the streets while on a bike. In most cities, the luxury of entitlement is reserved for automobile drivers. When driving my minivan in North America, like most other people, I get annoyed when cyclists take up space in my lane. When pedestrians jaywalk, I curse them under my breath for having the gall to come into my space. I am the master of the road, and I expect everyone else around me to bow to that. In Copenhagen, I had the same feeling, but I felt it on a bike. It may have been psychological as much as practical – maybe I was still feeling a little giddy over my cycle chic moment – but it felt like every other mode of transportation was subservient to me. Cars seemed to get the raw deal in many intersections. Pedestrians kept an eye out for me. I felt entitled to get where I wanted to go. It was difficult to believe the assertions by Rohl and Colville-Andersen that the city was dominated by cars only a couple of generations previously.

Things weren't perfect in Copenhagen, of course. There are still a lot of cars, and with them comes the associated noise, grit and sense of urgency. The sheer number of cyclists also creates its own problems. Bike parking can be tough to find, and a mass of thousands of bicycles is only slightly less unsightly than a mass of thousands of cars, even if it does take up less space. As a pedestrian, I also sometimes felt that bikes were out to get me – I was wary and alert while walking, which wasn't always a relaxing experience. On the whole, however, I liked what cycling brought to the city. It seemed to be returning a more humane scale to cities that have tended to outgrow us. In the overheated rhetoric around cycling these days it's easy to forget that the goal of bicycle advocacy isn't to get more people cycling. That's just the means to the end. The end is a better, healthier, more vibrant and efficient city. I saw glimpses of all that.

Near the end of my day exploring Copenhagen on a bike, I parked near the famous tourist strip Nyhavn, a waterfront canal district beloved by visitors for the colourful facades of the 17th- and 18th-century buildings and the tall wooden ships docked for display. Despite Melanie's warning, I couldn't resist the

Nyhavn tourist sausages (which, incidentally and perhaps fittingly, I ate almost directly across the canal from Noma, which had just been named the best restaurant in the world) when I realized that for most of the day, I hadn't given much thought to the weather. I had been outside riding a bike in temperatures below freezing for hours. My warm attire had gone on and off through the day, as the wind picked up or the sun came out, but for somebody who came to the city on a mission to explore winter, I realized that the season had barely crossed my mind. Maybe this is what Rohl and Colville-Andersen were talking about when they said most Copenhageners don't pay much mind to the weather when they are cycling. I thought they were downplaying the impacts of winter, but perhaps they were just articulating their own instincts, and those shared by thousands of other residents of this city, that bike-friendly cities are nearly immune to seasons. Riding a bike kept my internal furnace humming, the infrastructure kept me safe, and the hordes of cyclists all around me kept me from feeling like an anomaly. Would this approach work in cities where winter was harsher, such as Oulu or my own city of Calgary? It's difficult to say.

If I learned anything from my search for the

perfect winter cycling city, it's that there is no such thing, because there's no perfect winter and cities are as different as the winters that occur in them. So perhaps the real path to year-round cycling viability isn't to find the perfect city, but to build what is needed, specific to each city and each winter. If that's the case, there's no need to start from scratch. Cycling cities, it seems, are like families in that they are dysfunctional in their own ways, but the happy ones all share similar traits: an acknowledgement that cycling is good for cities and society, an appreciation for cycling as a viable form of transportation, encouragement for people of all ages to ride bikes, a rejection of cycling as a subculture, and perhaps most importantly, infrastructure and government policy that supports cycling. All of those points apply all the time, no matter the season.

As I munched my sausage, I saw two young Japanese women with clipboards on the street. They were stopping passersby to ask questions in accented English. I leaned within earshot, and realized the conversations were about cycling. When there was a lull in their work, I introduced myself as a journalist from Canada writing about cycling. Their faces lit up. They were on a similar mission. They were students of sustainability at the University of Tokyo, and were in Copenhagen to learn about ways of improving cycling. They were here asking people why they chose to ride a bike. Here was my chance, I thought, to swipe a bit of hard work from students; it would be like having my own intern. So, I wondered, what were the reasons? They giggled a bit, and then shared some of their research. Some people told the students they rode a bike because it improved their health. One person that day told them they rode a bike because it's good for the environment. But by far the most common answer was the simplest: riding a bike is the quickest and easiest way to get around the city. "Yeah," I said. "That's what everybody tells me too." We chatted a bit more, and I was about to leave when I asked them what people said about winter itself, whether the cold and snow stopped them from riding, or if the cold weather pushed them back into their cars. I had asked this question enough to know that most Danes would probably answer by saying winter is irrelevant to their cycling; that it was something they didn't think too much about. Still, it remained an issue in my mind, and I figured it was worth asking.

The students both stared at me with blank looks. "Oh," one of them said. "We didn't think to ask that."

SEASON THREE
THE ATTITUDE

CHAPTER 18

In 1956, deep into the Giro d'Italia, a professional bike race around Italy that is one of the sport's three grand tours, along with the Tour de France and La Vuelta España in Spain, a tiny, unpleasant Luxembourger named Charly Gaul entered a stage of the race minutes behind the leaders. He wasn't even in contention for the winner's pink jersey that morning – he sat well outside the top ten best cumulative times – but this was a mountain stage, heading up Monte Bondone, a 2000 metre peak in northern Italy, and Gaul was a climber, one of the best the sport had seen.

In professional bicycle racing, climbers are a different breed. Sprinters are bigger, stronger and have sexier jobs because they win a lot of stages, which puts them on television receiving kisses from podium girls. Come mountain stages, however, they end up being left far behind by the climbers. Usually small, and skilled in suffering, climbers tend to find ways into the hearts of fans because of the pain they endure to win. There often seems to be something driving a climber that goes beyond desire; something primal. Pathological competitiveness, in the case of Eddy Merckx, the greatest cyclist of all time. Daddy issues, perhaps, in the cases of Lance Armstrong and his nemesis Jan Ullrich. After winning three Tours de France, American Greg LeMond revealed a heartbreaking story of abuse as a child. All were strong climbers. Gaul was pushed by some inner demons too. Writer Philippe Brunel once speculated that Gaul was riding away from his modest upbringing in Luxembourg, trying to escape the mundane life that had been set out for him. Whatever drove him, it eventually took over his life. After his retirement from cycling, he turned into a hermit and spent his retirement years isolated and alone, his memory gone and his mind a doddering mess. Even during his racing days he was known among riders as a taciturn eccentric, prone to moodiness, rarely speaking to racers on other teams. A lazy pedaller on flat stages, he had another skill that stands out among the semi-mythical stories about the middle years of bike racing that persist today. Gaul was at his best when conditions were atrocious.

So when the snow started falling that day in 1956, Gaul was in his element. Unlike most riders of the day, Gaul tended to spin at a high cadence, locking into a small gear on the steep roads, spinning at a pace slightly higher than the rest, a style that was gently mocked at the time but was later adopted by Lance Armstrong. Snow isn't unusual during the Giro. Most years see at least a couple of stages come to an end at ski resorts that, even in May, remain buried under huge drifts. This year was different. After a few earlier climbs, Gaul suffered a flat tire and was trailing the leaders, but as the race hit the foot of the 14-kilometre climb up Monte Bondone, the insanity began. The stage should have been cancelled because of the worsening weather, but it wasn't. The temperature dropped, the wind picked up and riders headed into a full-scale blizzard. That's when Gaul made his move.

Slowly Gaul worked his way to the front of the pack. One by one, riders, cold and shivering, abandoned the race, dozens of them. The wind and cold were too much. Numb and blue, their limbs nearly frozen in place, some riders tried to warm up in pails of hot water offered by fans on the side of the road. Others simply leaned their bikes on a roadside tree and talked their way into warm farmhouses for some heat. By the end of the day, half of the racers had quit. Even Gaul himself went missing for a time. According to some reports, his race director in the tailing car lost sight of him and was desperately trying to find him amid the blowing snow when he spotted Gaul's bike leaning outside a roadside trattoria. When the director went inside, Gaul was there, his eyes blank from pain, his teeth chattering while he warmed himself with a cup of coffee. Knowing the state he was in, the team director spoke gently, rubbed warmth back into his muscles and guided him onto his bike. Soon, Gaul was back on the mountain, spinning at a murderous pace.

If anything, conditions got worse. After more than 200 kilometres of racing, the pink jersey holder quit with only two kilometres to go, unable to finish. Here's how *L'Équipe* writer Christophe Penot described the rest of the race:

> Charly Gaul, accompanied by two carabinieri (military police), his face deformed by cold-induced swelling, his lips thick and blue, as if ready to burst, and his eyes silent stammering cries of torment and fear. For, as sensational as he was on apocalyptic days, the Luxembourger thought for a while that he might not reach the summit, pedalling on autopilot without being able to fathom the stakes ... but who could understand?

Gaul just kept going. When he reached the summit, he was alone. He had won, not just the stage, but he had made up enough time to overtake the overall race leaders. The pink jersey was his. There's a famous photo of Gaul at the summit, being carried off his bike. His body seems frozen in riding position, his legs locked at the knee. His lips are swollen and his face is puffy from the cold. His eyes are dead, as if his brain disconnected from the conscious part of his psyche, leaving his body free to pedal unthinkingly amid the pain. Gaul went on to have more success in cycling – he won a Tour de France after a similarly heroic comeback amid horrendous conditions, and nearly a second save for a badly timed break to urinate one year that earned him the nickname Monsieur Pi-Pi – but that day on Monte Bondone defined his career and, considering the way his mind left him in later years, his life.

On some cold winter days while out riding, when things start to get bad, I think of Gaul. Thanks to the Weather Network and the Internet, I'm rarely in a similar situation to Gaul's that day, caught unprepared in a blizzard. But sometimes, as the winter wind cuts through my jacket as I climb out of the river valley on my way home from work, that image of Gaul at the top of Monte Bondone pops into my head. His swollen lips, his thin woollen jersey and shorts, the way his legs seem frozen in position – all of it serves not so much as an inspiration, but as a test. I imagine myself in his shoes that day in 1956, and I can't help but ask the questions. What would I have done? Would I have pushed myself the way he did? Would I have quit like so many riders that day? Why didn't Gaul just give up? He could have saved himself the torment and pain in the midst of a race nobody expected him to win anyway. What drove him?

Of course riding from work is not on the same scale as a 200-kilometre race through the Dolomites against the best athletes on the planet, but getting home some days is my Monte Bondone. It would be easy to quit and take refuge in a Starbucks and call my wife to pick me up. Nobody has any expectations of me finishing the ride, and nobody would ever blame me for abandoning it. But usually it takes only a few minutes for me to overcome those thoughts and make it home. In retrospect, once I warm up a bit, I find those moments of comparing myself to Gaul a tad dramatic, especially after travelling to those European hubs of winter cycling, where riding a bike in bad weather is more a matter of practicality than heroics – but they do make me wonder.

After several winters of cycling, I had made great strides in my quest to become an all-season cyclist. I had a winter bicycle I was happy with. I had ridden in the best winter cycling cities in the world. Through the writing on my blog, I had connected with many other cyclists in the city who took pride in winter riding. And I had grown to love it. Even those awful days, when the image of Charly Gaul popped into my head, finishing the ride filled me with energy and confidence, and was the best part of my work day. Just like in the summer, riding was keeping me fit without taking away time from my family to hit the gym, it was inexpensive, and it gave me a chance to explore my city, even in the quiet off-season. If I was forced to drive to work because of other commitments, I missed my bike and the good mood that came with it. I had turned into a devotee.

Even still, winter cycling was seen by most people as deranged. Co-workers thought me nuts, and had little hesitation in saying so. "Just drive your car," people said. "What's wrong with you?"

When I heard those comments during the first few seasons I rode, I secretly enjoyed them. They made me feel exceptional. I was doing something most people wouldn't even consider, and I liked the status it gave me. But after all I had gone through on my mission to discover the viability of winter cycling, such comments started to wear on me. I had spent so much time finding a good winter bike and I had seen the benefits of winter cycling in other cities, I started viewing others' judgments differently. If I could see the positive side of winter cycling, why couldn't they? Winter cycling makes so much sense on a personal and a macro level – it's good for society, it improves cities, untangles congestion, makes us more social, makes us healthy, is inexpensive personally and for governments, and is better for the environment – why was it still seen as something for radicals?

After all this time, I started looking at these questions differently. Maybe it wasn't the lack of a decent winter bike that was holding people back. Maybe it wasn't the friendliness of the city to bikes. Maybe the problem went a little deeper. Perhaps the story of the 1956 Giro d'Italia shouldn't have been about Charly Gaul's fortitude, but rather the lack of fortitude demonstrated by everyone else. Maybe, I thought, the problem facing winter cycling was us.

CHAPTER 19

There's a scene in *Fargo*, the great 1996 Coen brothers film, in which William H. Macy, playing an in-over-his-head car salesman who arranges the kidnapping of his wife to collect the ransom money, trudges out to the middle of an empty parking lot during the depths of a Midwestern winter. As he clears the snow from his car, the stress of his unravelling plan hits him, and he vents his frustration on the vehicle's windshield with a snowbrush.

It's a wonderful, emotional scene, and part of what makes it so powerful is the setting. That frozen, snow-blown prairie is such a force in the film that it's almost impossible to imagine the scene working as well in different weather. Winter becomes a metaphor for the bleakness of Macy's situation, compounding his desperation and hopelessness.

As I was thinking about the reasons we seem to hate winter, this scene struck me in a different way than it did the first time I had seen it. Pop culture both reflects our collective attitudes and influences them, so I started paying attention to the way winter is depicted in the media, movies, music and television. It's illuminating to look at the entertainment we consume through the lens of winter, and a little horrifying if you think our negative impressions of winter are holding us back from something positive like winter cycling.

What I first noticed about that scene in *Fargo* is the presence of winter at all. Despite the fact that winter occupies a good chunk of the year for tens of millions of North Americans, we almost never see winter reflected in popular culture. And when we do, it's almost never portrayed positively. Like the way it's used in *Fargo*, winter has become shorthand for all those emotions we hate: loneliness, bleakness, emptiness, and harshness.

In Stanley Kubrick's *The Shining*, winter is both an inescapable threat and a trap. It's what forces a stir-crazy Jack Nicholson into full-blown nutbar mode, and it's what keeps his family from escaping him. While winter does end up saving little Danny Lloyd's character by freezing his crazed father to death, who remembers that? The lasting image of the film is the insane winter isolation.

Star Wars Episode V: The Empire Strikes Back has the frozen planet of Hoth as, at first, a refuge for the rebel forces of Luke Skywalker and Han Solo, presumably because Darth Vader's cape isn't made of wool. But winter quickly becomes the enemy when Luke is attacked by a steroidal yeti and then nearly freezes to death, saved only by the warmth of the entrails from a fresh carcass.

In the adaptation of Stephen King's *Misery*, winter traps James Caan with a crazed fan played by Kathy Bates, a scenario that is just as plausible in the summer, but somehow not as frightening. There's a whole genre of horror films that use winter to chill us by trapping the heroes while death comes calling. John Carpenter's *The Thing* sets the action in Antarctica to make the whole thing seem even more claustrophobic and paranoid.

Frozen, the Disney film that's become the highest-grossing animated movie of all time, casts winter as the physical and emotional villain. Princess Elsa has the power to summon snow and ice at will, which goes awry when she storms off in a fit of anger, leaving the kingdom socked in by the mother of all blizzards. Only when she gets in touch with her emotions does the big melt begin. The movie not only makes winter out to be something to fear, it uses the season as a metaphor for suppressing your true self. Yeesh.

Where are the positive images of winter in the movies? Relegated to Christmas titles. About the only time we see lovely images of falling snow is in the denouements of holiday rom-coms, when everyone comes together for a hug and the sky drops lovely flakes of snow at exactly the right time to remind everyone of the real meaning of Christmas. (Note to Hollywood: to somebody who actually lives through winter, your fake snow looks like soap – is realistic-looking snow really so difficult?) There's nothing wrong with those moments, but why can't they happen in everyday movies? In the obligatory scenes of lovelorn leading men running to airports to stop perfectly coiffed and unusually understanding lovers from leaving, can they not take place in winter? In teen comedies, massive drunken parties when parents are out of town can just as easily happen in winter.

It's not just movies. Winter is also shorthand for heartbreak and loss in pop music, when it's mentioned at all. Few songs illustrate this as much as one of the more recent tunes from the folk-rock band The Avett Brothers, who have a song on their 2012 album *The Carpenter* called "Winter in My Heart" that begins with these lyrics: "It must be winter in my heart/ There's nothing warm in there at all." The song goes on to tell the story of a man so heartbroken that it feels like winter in his soul even when "the calendar says July 4." Among the more famous pop songs that mention winter include Simon and Garfunkel's "Hazy Shade of Winter," which offers up hopelessness and despair, but only until "The fields are ripe, it's the springtime of my life." In the Mamas and Papas' "California Dreaming," the lead character of the song is trapped where it's brown and grey, and can only solace himself by thinking of California, where it's "safe and warm." The Rolling Stones wrote about the season in one of their signature ballads called, aptly, "Winter," in which poor Mick seems to be having a tough time in the "cold, cold winter" when the "light of love is all burned out." And, because apparently people only fall in love during the months of spring and summer, Mick can only "hope it's gonna be a long, hot summer/ And the light of love will be burnin' bright."

It goes on and on. Perhaps the best example of our hate-on for winter is *The Lion, the Witch and the Wardrobe*, in which the fantastical land of Narnia is held in perpetual winter (but never Christmas) by the White Witch, who has a habit of freezing her enemies into stone. Only when the Christ-stand-in Aslan the Lion comes does the witch's spell start to break and the snow begin to melt. One winter, I paid attention to the number of television commercials set in winter. Outside of ads hawking Christmas, of which winter is little more than a backdrop, I only came across two, both of them negative. One was for winter tires that depicted the dire consequences of having the gall to use all-season tires in snow. The other involved a homeowner reluctantly starting up his snow blower while dreaming of a tropical vacation.

Many of these examples illustrate one of the key uses of winter as a metaphor. It is often used to represent a lack of feeling and emotionlessness. Which is strange considering the strong feelings we have towards winter. We hate it. We hate it so much that we seem to be trying to collectively will it away. In our popular culture, art and literature, we are increasingly ignoring it, as if it doesn't even exist. According to Google's Ngram Viewer, which indexes millions of books from 1800 to 2000, the number of times the word "winter" appeared in books has steadily fallen. Mentions of the word "snow" peaked around 1900 and have declined without fail. Even the word "cold," which has many meanings, has been falling steadily since the 1870s. Conversely, the words "summer" and "beach" have been steadily growing in use.

Those numbers also confirm something else. We didn't always despise winter. For much of the 18th and 19th centuries, there was a kind of awe of winter, in which those who bested it were venerated. You can see this in the way that golden age explorers were turned into heroes of the day, even when they failed spectacularly, as was the case with British adventurer Robert Falcon Scott, whose quest to be the first to the South Pole ended when he arrived to find Norwegian Roald Amundsen had beaten him to it by a matter of weeks. Even though Scott and his four companions perished on the return journey due to a mixture of starvation, cold and, some might say, hubris, he remains a top-shelf British hero. We still hold in high regard those who, by sheer human will (and a little help from technology and Sherpas), overcome the cold on the slopes of Mount Everest every year, even when climbing the world's highest peak has become a bit of an absurd undertaking. Those who manage to survive when lost in the winter woods are still newsworthy, as are the bumbling blokes from the British automobile/comedy series *Top Gear* when they become the first to drive a vehicle to the North Pole.

Beyond that, however, there was a kind of romance to winter in times past. In his collection of essays titled *Winter*, writer Adam Gopnik recalls historical moments in which winter was seen as a recuperative season. From the late 1700s to the middle of the 20th century, there's little doubt winter was more difficult than it is today because of advances in clothing and central heating, but there is a sense of winter reflected in the art, music and literature of the time as a season of renewal, comfort and, believe it or not, pleasure. He quotes the classical composer Vivaldi, whose endlessly popular *Four Seasons* includes a violin paean to icy rain and who also wrote poems about the joy of slip-sliding on winter's ice, which "gladdens one's heart." During the Napoleonic era, Gopnik notes the embracing of winter was a kind of German nationalism, something to buttress the country against the incoming French, who hailed from a country that lacked the harsher climate of its northern neighbour. Not every depiction of winter was positive – perhaps the most popular winter painting of all time, Gopnik points out, may be Caspar David Friedrich's "The Sea of Ice" that depicts sea ice crushing an unfortunate ship – but there was a romanticism of winter in the work of artists from northern Europe to Japan. As recently as the Canadian Group of Seven painters, winter was depicted in romantic ways, with beautiful stylized images of icebergs and nation-defining snow-capped mountains.

Such depictions today, however, are rare, resulting in a decline in that kind of romantic sensibility concerning winter in contemporary culture. What we are left with is, as Patrick Coleman of the Winter Cities Institute once told me, is an aspiration for all of us to live in California. We are inundated with such ideas: reality-television shows filmed in sunny Los Angeles, palm-trees and cherry-red convertibles in our movies, summertime in the flyover states in our television dramas. The barrage of sunniness is literal and figurative, but it's not coincidental. We are presented with pleasant images of warmth because it makes us feel good, and which makes us easy targets for sales pitches or narrative emotional climaxes. It also, however, seems to build up in us a desire for more, a kind of self-fulfilling prophecy. If we never see images of winter, why would we seek them out? I don't want to overstate the influence of media images on our perceptions of the places we live – the experience of one blizzard will do far more damage to our attempts to embrace winter than a lifetime of scenes of bikini beaches in magazine ads – but they aren't without impact. They tend to push aside the positive images of winter we carry around in our heads: those moments of skating on a pond on a crisp day, or building snowmen with our kids or, perhaps, the perfect bicycle ride through the snow in favour of those emphasizing both ugliness and cold.

The question for now is: what happened? How did we lose sight of the positive side of winter?

CHAPTER 20

In 2001, researchers in several winter countries got together to study a simple but rarely explored question: what do children think of winter? Or, more technically, they wanted to look at "schoolchildren's adaptation to winter in cold climates." The goal was to better understand the way kids adapt to winter so programs could be designed to get them outside and active all year round. A questionnaire was developed and presented to kids in Canada, Japan and Finland, to gauge their attitudes toward winter. "If we had activities in the urban outdoors for one or more weeks during the cold season and enjoyed outdoor activities, we could reduce the length of winter in our mind through enjoying outdoor play and other forms of winter activity," the report stated.

The study posed questions that asked children to rank their perceptions of winter, using such terms as "I hate winter" or "I usually don't like winter," to "I sometimes like winter" or "I love winter." For the sake of comparison, adults in all three countries were also asked the same questions.

The results were slightly different in each country, and offer much insight into our attitudes toward winter. Generally, the study found that children have much more positive attitudes toward winter than adults, but that positive outlook slowly fades as they age. In Canada, kids were split almost evenly between those who said they hate winter, and those who said they love winter. In Japan, among seven- and eight-year-olds, nearly 40 per cent of children said they love winter, compared to only 5 per cent who said they hate winter.

In Japan, the children were also asked how much time they spent outside playing in winter. The more time a child spent outside, the more likely they were to say they liked winter. "There is a relationship between the amount of time playing outdoors and the rates of positive adaptation replies to winter."

Interestingly, in all these countries, by adulthood attitudes toward winter changed dramatically. By their 20s and 30s, people in all the countries were clearly suffering through winter or at least tolerating it. The most common response in all adults in the study was "hate." As my mother used to say, "hate" is a pretty strong word.

I can't say the results of this study were a surprise to me. In fact, they solidified what I had already learned after a lifetime living in a winter climate: kids tend to like winter because they see it as fun. And if you look at winter with the perspective of a child, it is a blast. After big wet snowfalls, my kids can't wait to get outside and play. They know it's cold, but they dress for it and make it work. Experiences like that made me wonder why all of us don't get outside to enjoy winter more often even though it's easy to see why. We have become masters at avoidance. In northern climates, we have become so adept at circumventing winter that we no longer have any connection to it. It's become little more than a nuisance.

That's not necessarily a bad thing. Life has become much easier since the days of Laura Ingalls Wilder's *The Long Winter*, when blizzards stranded towns without food for months at a time, forcing them to survive on potatoes and bread while staying warm by burning pyres of twisted hay. Or Wilder's Canadian equivalent, Susanna Moodie, whose *Roughing It in the Bush* portrays a truly horrific winter life in the mid-1800s, with tales of nearly frozen babies, starving cattle and harrowing loneliness.

These days, the western world has managed to remove nearly all of the danger from winter. We move from heated homes to heated cars to heated offices and back, with only fleeting moments outside. Even within those parameters things have got easier. Home heating and insulation are better and less expensive than ever, at least in newer homes equipped with natural gas furnaces and high-tech stuffing in their walls. My expat hosts in Denmark moved to the country confident that the milder European winter would be easy to take after a lifetime of harsh Canadian winters, but holed up in a drafty 100-year-old home with massively expensive oil heaters, they were reduced to using a wood-burning stove to stave off the shivers. It was so tough to stay warm, they actually missed winter in Canada. There are plenty of homes in North America that still use heating oil, although high-quality natural gas networks have made it around to many cities, making cold weather much more bearable, but also more easily avoided.

Our cars have also gotten better in the winter. Improvements in snow tires, the addition of anti-lock brakes, and even fuel injection have all reduced the struggles of winter driving, which was once a harrowing experience. Cars were reluctant to start, they wouldn't brake on ice and heaters were notoriously fickle. All of that has changed. It's not just more convenient to drive in winter these days, it's safer. Overall, the rate of traffic fatalities in the U.S. has dropped from more than five deaths per 100 million vehicle miles travelled in the 1960s to less than 1.5 today (although there were still a truly stunning 40,000 U.S. traffic fatalities in 2007). The number of Canadians who died in traffic collisions declined by more than 50 per cent from the late 1970s to the mid-2000s. Despite this, we still think of winter driving as the most dangerous thing most of us do in our lives. Contrary to common perceptions, the winter months are not when most fatal traffic accidents occur. The most dangerous month on North American highways is August, during the busy summer holiday season, according to both the U.S. National Highway Traffic Safety Administration and Statistics Canada. The depths of winter between January and April actually record the fewest fatalities. Believe it or not, snowstorms are among the safest days to be on roads. While the number of collisions increases, those collisions aren't as dangerous because people tend to slow down. All of this means surviving winter has gotten easier over the years, but it also means we don't have to deal with the problems that it creates like we once did. This reduces winter from something we must face head-on to little more than an inconvenience, yet our perceptions about the danger and harshness of winter persist.

In many cities, we've taken the view that winter is something to be avoided to the extreme. Dozens of North American cities have, over the years, built networks of interconnected tunnels or skywalks to help people stay indoors as much as possible. They range from small offshoots of the subway system in New York to the famous "underground city" in Montreal, now known as the RÉSO, which stretches for 32 kilometres under downtown and features everything from shopping centres to banks and museums. City statistics say more than 500,000 people use the heated and well-lit system in Montreal, with use peaking in the winter. In Calgary, where I live, much of the downtown is connected through a network of enclosed bridges or skywalks, known as plus-15s, because most are 15 feet above the ground. The first was built in 1970, and the system now numbers nearly 60 bridges stretching 16 kilometres, making it one of the longest such systems in the world. Ask nearly any Calgarian downtown worker in the middle of winter what they think of the plus-15s, and they'll gush like a smitten teenager – business meetings can be taken without winter jackets, and lunch can be found without having to bundle up and face the weather. What's not to love?

Despite that love, however, there are problems created by such systems. Not only are they criticized by urbanists for hurting the street life of cities – in Calgary, downtown streets are all but devoid of life in the winter – but they also change our relationship with the season on a less tangible level. When you can spend your whole day in the middle of February without encountering the weather, what does that do to your perceptions of it? For that matter, when we can spend nearly an entire season indoors, what does the outdoors come to mean? Winter becomes disconnected from our lives. It becomes The Other, an ethereal villain that exists only to trouble us. The result can be seen in the study mentioned earlier: avoidance begets hate.

This may be most obvious in Canada. There was a time when Canadians considered themselves winter people. In the 1800s, winter was one of the defining characteristics of the country. Winter was something to be embraced and enjoyed. In Montreal, among the most exclusive cliques in the city were snowshoeing clubs, where the elite would gather to socialize and make decisions about the city (excluding, of course, the First Nations people who invented snowshoeing), kind of like golfing today. Nearly any-body who could afford it would have a portrait pho-tograph taken while wearing their finest winter furs, which makes for quaint but bizarre-looking pictures today. Turn-of-the-20th-century photographs from the west feature intrepid families donning ice skates and going for sleigh rides. Compared to most of the dour-looking expressions on people's faces in most of the portraits of the day, winter looked like a mag-ical time of frivolity.

In the big eastern cities of the country, winter fes-tivals were hugely popular events in the late 1800s. In 1884, word of the second instalment of the Montreal Winter Carnival had spread as far as New York. *The New York Times* published a glowing preview of the event, writing of "an Ice Palace in Dominion-square, parades, races, fire-works, and all sorts of jollity." Wealthy New Yorkers, including the Vanderbilts, made plans to attend. In 1885 in Montreal, architect A.C. Hutchison, famous for his 1860–62 stone work on the East Block of Canada's Parliament build-ings, was commissioned to design an ice castle for the winter carnival. This was no snow fort. At 100 feet high, and illuminated "by electricity," the behe-moth made headlines far and wide. In 1887 the cas-tle was built big enough to accommodate a rink used for pleasure skating and hockey games. To help celebrate that year, organizers invited American military expert Capt. Arthur L. Howard, who had developed the nickname "Gat" when he was sent north by Dr. Richard Gatling with a pair of his then famous Gatling machine guns to help put down the Northwest Rebellion of Métis leader Louis Riel two years before. Howard brought a gun to Montreal, hauled it to the top of the main tower and fired a volley of fireworks to applause below. Festival organizers even defied nature by building an artificial hill that was lit up at night for the use of people on sleds and toboggans.

Similar carnivals popped up in other cities, becoming one of the bright spots on the annual calendar. Alas, the winter frivolity did not last. Despite the popularity of winter carnivals, they were soon ended by officials, including famed railway builder William Van Horne, who thought the festivals were becoming too popular, believing that the image of winter was limiting Canada's tourism opportunities. Tourism brochures soon gave up frozen images for something now seen as quintessentially Canadian: majestic mountain ranges and railroads winding through endless summer forests, with nary a snowflake to be seen. It wasn't until the 1950s that

Quebec City's Winter Carnival returned as an annual event.

In some ways, the decline of the early incarnations of the winter carnivals also heralded the end of Canadians as a true winter people. Today, almost every adult I know says they hate winter, and it's not just Canada. There was once a kind of perverse pride among winter people in North America; those who were hardy enough to withstand it fancied themselves stronger for it. Now, we leave that to other nations, with the possible exception of Alaskans and Winnipeggers. Our forte is complaining. We've become experts in kvetching about the weather. During a winter storm, no matter how mild, online social media becomes a cavalcade of bellyaching and exaggeration, in which an overnight dumping that might once have been seen as a healthy sign of winter is transformed into "snowmageddon" or "snowpocalypse." The U.S. Weather Channel in 2013 decided to start naming winter storms in the style of hurricanes, which at first seemed like a joke (the inaugural season of names included such villainous sounding sci-fi geekery as Draco, Khan and Xerxes – try to say "winter storm Xerxes" with a straight face), but soon took off, to the delight, no doubt, of the Weather Channel's marketing department. The criteria for a storm being named, according to the company's Tom Nizol, was: "The process for naming a winter storm will reflect a more complete assessment of several variables that combine to produce disruptive impacts including snowfall, ice, wind and temperature. In addition, the time of day (rush hour vs. overnight) and the day of the week (weekday school and work travel vs. weekends) will be taken into consideration in the process the meteorological team will use to name storms." With such broad criteria, it's easy to see how storms that were once a regular part of winter life (and, for skiers, a highlight of the year) will now become events of fear. Who can you blame for ruining your commute? Winter storm Khan. Khaaaan!

Even the number of people enjoying winter outdoor activities is disturbingly flat or declining. The estimated number of visits to U.S. ski areas in 2011 and 2012, for example, was nearly identical to the number in 1979, despite huge population growth. In Canada, the size of the "snowsports" market, which includes all kinds of skiing and snowboarding, declined to 2.3 million active participants in 2010–11, from 2.7 million active participants in 2001–02. While that doesn't necessarily mean the number of people who hate winter is increasing, it does mean the number of people taking part in winter-only sports is declining, and those people tend to be the ones who say they enjoy winter the most. And some of our most popular winter sports have gone indoor as well – hockey, figure skating and curling are no more winter sports than swimming or basketball are now summer sports. The competitions and practices are almost exclusively held indoors year-round, so the weather has no bearing on any of them unless one is caught in a snowstorm on the way.

All of this may have been inevitable. It's difficult to find fault with making life more comfortable in winter, especially for seniors and those most vulnerable. Who in their right mind would want to reverse these trends? "Sorry, grandma, you'll have to walk through that snowstorm because the underground tunnel has been closed for your own good." Even those who enjoy the outdoors in winter benefit from the current trend. Winter clothing is warmer and lighter today than ever before, a boon for skiers and snowboarders. If he were alive and making a push to the top of Everest today, I'm sure George Mallory would gladly trade his turn-of-the-20th-century woollen leggings for the information-age super-fabrics that warm modern mountaineers in freezing death zones. You'd have to be a masochist to reject the progress that's made winter more bearable over the years.

But does embracing that progress mean we must also reject winter? If we've been so successful at mitigating winter as a significant factor in daily existence, can we not also find ways to make being outside in winter more bearable? Or, put another way, can we not find a place for winter in our lives? An attitude of acceptance, rather than avoidance, it turns out, may be the real key to making winter cycling a viable transportation and recreation alternative in North America. Although for that, we may have to look elsewhere for guidance.

CHAPTER 21

In 1858, the Journal of the Statistical Society published a study that examined fluctuations in the number of deaths throughout Britain at different times of the year. Examining statistics from around the country, the study didn't make any grand conclusions, but may have been the first to put some science behind what was no doubt a trend that had been noticed since *Homo sapiens* left Africa for chillier parts of the world: people die at different rates in winter. The study author seemed more concerned, with good reason considering the time at which he was writing, about the way English cesspools spread disease, but it's an interesting glimpse into a question that was asked in several more studies more than 100 years later, when the impacts of climate change started to become a concern.

In 2008, a group of scientists working out of the University of Athens looked more deeply at what the authors call the "paradox of excess winter mortality." In other words, the study set out to determine if it was true that, strangely, more people die from the effects of winter in countries with the mildest winters. "The paradox consists of the fact that higher mortality rates are generally found in less severe, milder winter climates where, all else equal, there should be less potential for cold strain and cold related mortality," the study authors wrote.

An examination of data over ten years from 15 different European cities showed that the highest proportion of people killed by the elements in winter were from Portugal, Spain and Ireland, where winters are, compared to the colder Scandinavian countries, mostly mild. The reason? The authors suggested a simple one: these people weren't prepared for harsher weather. Housing in those countries tends to lack winter insulation, and home heating isn't adequate, something the authors describe as "poor domestic thermal efficiency." You might say that winter kills people in places where winter is least expected.

Here's another way of looking at the issue. In 1998, three scientists in the U.K., Germany and Russia examined how cold winters impacted the health of senior citizens. The scientists went to Yekaterinburg, Russia, an industrial city deep in the Urals of Siberia, named after the wife of Peter the Great, which may be best known as the city where the Bolsheviks murdered Tsar Nicholas II and his family after the October Revolution. If you're studying the effects of winter, it's a good choice. It's cold. Damn cold, with a six-month winter and an average January high of $-9°C$ ($15.8°F$).

The authors set out to discover who, directly or indirectly, died of cold in the winter, and to interview senior citizens about the ways they dealt with the cold season. They encountered a problem with the first part of their study, however, when they couldn't find anybody who died as a result of the winter weather. Despite the downright frigid climate, with temperature drops far beyond those that killed people in milder western and southern Europe, "there was no increase in mortality in the population of an industrialized region of western Siberia as the temperature fell."

Thankfully, for the scientists at least, the interview portion went better. After surveying 167 seniors in the area and crunching the data, the study authors came to some startling conclusions. So what secret do Siberians harbour to keep them alive in the dead of winter? How do they manage to survive one of the coldest seasons on the planet, even as they age into a more vulnerable time in their lives? "Warm clothing and physical activity prevented cold stress outdoors and warm housing prevented cold stress indoors." In other words, when the temperature started dropping, seniors stayed safe outdoors by dressing warmly and exercising. When indoors, they warmed their houses sufficiently. The authors even managed to offer some advice to those milder countries that suffer winter deaths, which, one assumes, they didn't mean in a patronizing way, despite how it reads now: "These results suggest that the high excess winter mortality in western Europe could be prevented by people wearing sufficient clothing and engaging in physical activity outdoors, and by adequately heating houses."

That may be the biggest no-brainer study in history, but it does offer some insight into the way people tend to react to winter, and on another level, into winter cycling. In some colder climates, people tend to accept winter as a basic reality and adjust their lives accordingly. It might be overstating things to say they embrace winter, but there's a practicality to their existence that makes winter bearable. In those areas where winter is less harsh, and less consistent, such as those countries in Europe where winter mortality was highest, people are simply unprepared. It's easy to understand why, especially in places such as Spain and Portugal that experienced the higher winter mortality rates, because those blasts of winter were few and far between. In Siberia, winter settles in at the same time every year and doesn't leave for six months, so pretending it doesn't exist isn't an option.

The studies also struck me in another, perhaps less scientific way. After a lifetime of North American winters, I think our success in mitigating the season has, over the years, changed our attitudes toward it. We've moved from that more Russian attitude of acceptance and practicality, towards one that fits better with western Europe. On any cold winter day at a bus stop in Calgary, you can see teenagers huddled together wearing T-shirts and sneakers and nothing on their heads to keep warm lest it mess their hair. They act as if winter doesn't exist. Why? Because they are able to. Those few fleeting moments at the bus stop are likely the only moments of the day those teenagers will face the cold. They wake in homes with central heating, step into a warm bus, and spend their days basking in forced air warmed by natural-gas furnaces. One shouldn't read too much into the decisions of teenagers, but this image always strikes me as symbolic of our denial of winter. We've become so good at suppressing winter that we barely acknowledge its existence anymore. This rejection of nature might seem impractical but it's possible because of the ways we've managed to adjust our lives to remove the effects of winter. I know grown adults who don't own winter boots. Eventually, you'd think they would have to go outside, if not for practical reasons then at least for their own health, but I see people who spend weeks without going outside for pleasure. I'd argue this is one of the reasons we tend to hate winter so much, not because of the cold but because we feel cooped up for so long. Is being stir-crazy better than being cold? It's a tradeoff that seems to have a profound impact on our perceptions.

The way we've mastered the avoidance of winter also seems to have changed our perspective on it. We tend to remember the worst times – the blizzards and cold snaps that we were forced to confront, even if only when walking from the front door to the warmed-up SUV out front – but not the normal times. When thinking about winter, it looms large in our mind as a time of horrid cold and snow. While there are certainly times like that, we rarely look back with fondness on those lovely winter days when the temperature is mild, the sky clear under a brilliant sun, or when the snow is fluffy and inviting.

This selective memory that most of us display colours our view of the entire season, which impacts cycling as well. The biggest deterrent to winter cycling from the people I've spoken with is the cold (even though that may be the easiest thing to deal with simply by dressing for it). Those perceptions, however, seem off. Is it really as cold as we make it out to be?

During my first season of winter cycling, I set an arbitrary limit for myself: if it dropped below -10°C (14°F), I would drive my car. I thought it was just too cold and risky. It didn't take long, however, for me to adjust that cold threshold because I found I could easily stay warm at even colder temperatures. Soon, that number had dropped to -15°C (5°F) and then -20°C (-4°F), and I felt great. Interestingly, with that basement number in mind, I found there were actually very few days in which it was too cold to ride.

Most cities are this way. Sure, winter can bring some harsh days. But most are not too cold for some time outside, especially if your legs are pedalling enough to generate your own heat. In my city, I started asking people to guess the average temperature during the coldest winter months of January, February and March. Most guessed around -15°C (5°F). Some, acknowledging Calgary's regular warming winds, bumped that up to -10°C (14°F). I wouldn't have argued with either guess. Looking back at a lifetime of winters, what I remember is that time during college it dropped so cold that I kept the engine running while I pumped gas because I was afraid it wouldn't start again. When I went to pay, I received a tongue lashing from the gas jockey accusing me of trying to blow him up. I remember the spring blizzard that dumped so much heavy wet snow that I shovelled my roof lest it collapse under the weight. I remember school days that were so cold we struggled to do anything but organize a day-long game of floor hockey in the gymnasium because so few students and teachers showed up (snow days are for Hollywood; school was rarely cancelled for weather where I grew up).

So even I was surprised when I started gathering some data on winter temperatures. In Calgary, the violently cold winters of my mind actually have an average temperature for January, February and March of a paltry -4.84°C (23.28°F). I was almost insulted when I first saw those numbers. That's hardly winter. At that temperature, you barely need a winter jacket. A brisk walk is enough to keep you warm. What happened to the harsh winter by which I had defined myself? Like most Canadians, I tend to take a kind of perverse pride in my ability to withstand winter. I like to feel like I'm tougher than those soft southerners who fly into a panic when a dusting of snow hits their city. With such mild average temperatures, however, I felt embarrassed that the cold days loomed so large in my mind.

After seeing those numbers for Calgary, I decided to look up the winter temperatures of other cities. I knew the warm chinook winds of Calgary are an anomaly, so surely average winter temperatures must be harsher in other cities. Turns out, that's true. Winter is colder elsewhere in Canada (except in Toronto and Vancouver, where winters are milder: -3.3°C (26.06°F) in Toronto and 5.54°C (41.97°F) in Vancouver). Other average temperatures were not as cold as I expected. Edmonton, the most northerly big city in Canada, gets down to an average of -8.7°C (16.34°F) and Montreal hits -8.23°C (17.2°F). While colder, that average is still far from my winter-cycling comfort level temperature of about -20°C (-4°F), which is handled with little more than some thermal underwear, a few warm base layers, gloves and a balaclava. Even the prairie city of Winnipeg, which often boasts of being the coldest capital city in the world (a dubious honour challenged only by Ulan Bator, Mongolia) has a nearly manageable average temperature of -11.79°C (10.78°F).

Averages, of course, can be deceiving. Pulling down those numbers are those especially cold days in which the temperature hits -30°C (-22°F) or colder, but conversely, there are also days that pull the average temperature up. If we assume that winter is colder than it really is, it's the days with brilliantly bright winter sunlight and warming winds that we tend to forget about, not those with grisly cold.

Similar trends can be seen in American cities. Using the 2012 list of America's most bicycle-friendly cities compiled by *Bicycling* magazine, which measures dozens of U.S. municipalities for such factors as the percentage of bicycle commuters and the amount of bike infrastructure, I looked up the average temperatures of January, February and March. Here are the results, in order in which they ranked on the magazine's list (city stats weren't available for each burgh, so I included state-wide averages in some cases as marked):

Minneapolis-St. Paul: -9°C (15.8°F)
Portland, Oregon (statewide): 2.3°C (36.1°F)
Boulder, Colorado (statewide): -1.9°C (28.6°F)
Seattle, Washington (statewide): 1.8°C (35.2°F)
Eugene, Oregon (statewide): 2.3°C (36.1°F)
San Francisco, California (statewide): 8.7°F (47.7°F)
Madison, Wisconsin: (statewide): -6.6°C (20.1°F)

Bike infrastructure in Copenhagen, Denmark, February 2013.

Dog team and bicycle rider at Nome (Alaska), ca. 1901.

No. 638,575.

W. GUAY.
ICE VELOCIPEDE.
(Application filed Jan. 26, 1899.)

Patented Dec. 5, 1899.

(No Model.)

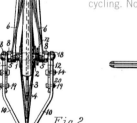

Fig. 1.

Fig. 3.

Fig. 2.

Ice Velocipede
Wilfrid Guay's "ice velocipede" from 1899.
This U.S. Patent Office drawing shows
one of many designs intended for winter
cycling. None ever found mass success.

Witnesses
S. Sweeney.
Dexter E. Tilley.

Inventor
Wilfrid Guay
by Allen Webster
Attorney

THE NORRIS PETERS CO., PHOTO-LITHO., WASHINGTON, D. C.

G. W. VAUGHAN.
ICE BICYCLE.
APPLICATION FILED APR. 10, 1905.

Ice Bicycle

Another ice bicycle
design, patented by
inventor
George W.
Vaughan
in 1905.

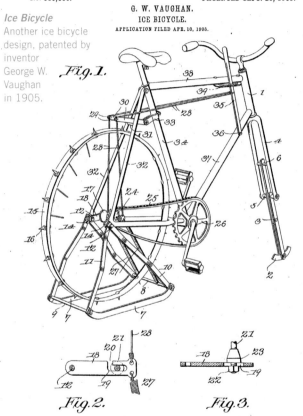

Fig. 1.

Fig. 2.   *Fig. 3.*

George W. Vaughan,
Inventor.

by

Attorneys

Top: *Jääkäri*

This model, the Jääkäri, from Finnish bike maker Helkama, is the same version used by the Finnish military, famously put to good use when fighting off invading Nazis and Soviets during the Second World War. PHOTO HELKAMA

Salsa Mukluk
This fat bike from Salsa Cycles is one of many
that have hit the mass market since the Alaskans
developed the idea. PHOTO SALSA CYCLES

Bottom Left: *Fat bike*
One of Mark Gronewald's early fat bike designs from his Alaska
company called Wildfire Designs. He and a number of Alaskan
cyclists tinkered with the design for years in order to incorporate
the massive tires to more easily get through snow and ice.
This model dates from around 2001. PHOTO MARK GRONEWALD

Cycle Chic
The original "Cycle Chic" photograph from Copenhagen,
Denmark (November 15, 2006). PHOTO MIKAEL COLVILLE-ANDERSEN

I also checked the average winter temperatures for these cities in the U.S., which are also known to be strong cycling centres:

New York City: 2.3°c (36.1°F)
Tucson, Arizona (statewide): 7.6°c (45.7°F)
Chicago, Illinois (statewide): 0°c (32°F)
Missoula, Montana (statewide): -4.7°c (23.5°F)
Marquette, Michigan (statewide): -4.8°c (23.4°F)
Anchorage, Alaska: -6°c (21.2°F)

Cold? Sure, but not painfully cold. Certainly nothing like Yekaterinburg, Russia. Certainly nothing that can't be dealt with. And certainly nothing that would stop a cyclist on most days, given some warm clothing, some studded tires and a little determination to squeeze every moment of bike fun out of the year.

I learned a couple of interesting things from these numbers. For one, winter may not be as bad as we think it is. In my experience, getting outside when the temperature is as cold as -10°c (14°F) is little more than an inconvenience. A warm jacket, hat and boots will keep you comfortable without too much consternation. Temperatures down to -20°c (-4°F) are also possible to deal with by seriously bundling up, limiting your time outdoors and ensuring you stay moving. It's possible to stay outside for much longer in colder temperatures, and thousands of outdoor workers prove this every day of the winter, but that is probably most people's limit. So to see the coldest temperature on that list at –9°C (15.8°F) shows that perhaps winter isn't as unfeasible on a bike as we may think.

It's also telling that Minneapolis–St. Paul, named America's best bike city, is also the coldest city on the list. This does much to disprove the notion that winter cities can't also be friendly to bicycles. Looking at the other cities on the list of most bike-friendly, there are some seriously cold climes represented. Madison, Wisconsin, only a four-hour drive from Minneapolis–St. Paul, likewise famous for its cold winters, also made the list. It's also worth noting that Anchorage, Alaska, no doubt a winter city in most people's minds, also has a reputation as an emerging bike city, and boasts an average winter temperature of only –6°C (21.2°F). This tells us two things about winter cycling: that we probably let our perceptions of cold discourage us too much from cycling; and that the severity of winter has little bearing on a city's bike friendliness.

Still, there are moments of cold in every city that can't be denied. In most discussions about winter cycling, somebody inevitably asks me what happens when the temperature falls to -30°C (-22°F). This seems to be the ultimate freezing point in most people's minds; the time when winter exists not just to inconvenience us, but to harm us. At this point, winter becomes hostile and dangerous. At least, it does so in our minds. Riding a bike at this temperature is impossible, right?

I'd say that's partially true. While it's still possible to ride in weather this cold – and there is a core group of riders who do so in just about every city – it's certainly not easy. Dressing warmer works, and once you get moving your body stays toasty, but -30°C (-22°F) seems to be the spot where most people's fear of the cold is overwhelming, no matter how much you try to convince them otherwise. It's also colder than I will usually ride, mostly out of respect for my wife's fear that I'll end up a frigid carcass on the edge of the road somewhere because of a flat tire. So, for the sake of argument, let's say -30°C (-22°F) is the absolute zero of winter cycling, the point where arguing in favour of the act is futile in the face of humanity's primal fear. Even if you are a dedicated bike commuter, you are most likely driving your car or taking public transit on these days.

Yet, the statistics also defy this kind of thinking. According to Environment Canada, between the years of 1981 and 2010, the average number of days in which the daily minimum temperature was colder than -30°C (-22°F) in Calgary for the entire year was 3.73. That means there are fewer than four days in the average year in which the temperature is too cold to contemplate riding. Also, that number represents, not the average temperature, but the low temperature for the day. That means rides during the day, especially that commute home in the late afternoon or early evening, could be much warmer.

Even if you are, like me, less hardy than that, the numbers are still illustrative. If we raise the absolute zero winter-cycling temperature to a more reasonable -20°C (-4°F), there are still only 21.7 days in which it would be too cold to ride in Calgary. How about -10°C (14°F), a temperature in which even the softest winter hater could manage quality time in the outdoors with little more than a pair of decent mittens and a warm hat? In Calgary, that would be 71.27 days a year. Even the wimpiest commuter could still be reasonably expected to ride their bike nearly ten months of the year.

Similar numbers play out in other cities as well.

Edmonton: 10.1 days at –30°C (–22°F), 36.77 days at
   –20°C (–4°F), 98.83 days at –10°C (14°F).
Winnipeg: 12.63 days at –30°C (–22°F), 51.98 days at
   –20°C (–4°F), 102.24 days at –10°C (14°F).
Toronto: zero days at –30°C (–22°F), 1.22 days at
   –20°C (–4°F), 21.86 days at –10°C (14°F).
Montreal: 0.44 days at –30°C (–22°F), 19.38 days at
   –20°C (–4°F), 69.29 days at –10°C (14°F).

American cities are similarly devoid of a huge
number of very cold days (depending, of course,
on your perception of "very cold"). Let's take
Minneapolis–St. Paul, the coldest, snowiest, most
wintry big metropolitan centre in the U.S. The mean
number of days in which the temperature dropped
to –17°C (1.4°F), the coldest such measurement provided by the National Oceanic and Atmospheric
Administration, in a year is 22.7. So if you are hardy
enough to ride when the thermometer bottoms out,
there are only 22.7 days of the year in which it will
be too cold for you. Granted, that's an extreme temperature, especially with the wet, cold and snowy
conditions of the region. Minneapolis–St. Paul has
147.6 days of the year in which the temperature is at
or below the freezing point of 0°C (32°F). Rare is the
winter-city-dweller who can't get in a little outdoor
time at that temperature, so let's say the number of

days in which it's too cold to ride exists somewhere between those two temperatures. If we pick the middle point, that gives cyclists about 73 days in the average year in which it is too cold to ride, a little more than ten weeks.

By those numbers, even in the coldest, most wintry big city in the U.S., there are 42 weeks of decent cycling weather. Such numbers are a bit of an eye-opener for those fearful of the cold weather, and those who argue against bike infrastructure in winter cities as a waste of money because nobody will use it year round (notwithstanding the fact that we spend taxpayer money all the time on stuff that sits idle for most of the year, from snowplows and lawn mowers to street lights which are switched off during the day). Still, our perceptions have a big influence on the number of people willing to take a chance on winter cycling. That winter of our minds, the one with killing frosts and huge snowstorms, may be an exaggeration.

There may also be a cultural side to this winter attitude. While there are obviously people in North America who know how to deal with winter, a different general attitude struck me most while in Europe. In Oulu, Finland, I asked almost everyone I met what they thought about winter. Back home, such

questions no doubt would generate scowls and pro-
testations of hate. But the most common initial reaction in Finland was a look of mild confusion. It
was almost as if people had never given the question
much thought; as if it was silly to form an opinion
on something you can't control, like asking what you
thought about the colour of the sky. After a little
prodding, most would shrug and answer with some
form of "what are you going to do?" A few of the
more thoughtful ones said something like, "I don't
love it, of course, but I do like having four seasons."
Almost all of them wondered why I, as a Canadian
raised in winter just like them, would be so interested in the their attitude toward winter. "Did you
just move there?" one person asked me.

In Denmark, I found a similar practicality: winter
didn't seem to be the enemy; it just was. It happened,
and you coped. On snow days, the streets were filled
with people on bicycles bundled in scarves and
woollen hats. Winter wasn't something to avoid;
it was just something to plan for. Mikael Colville-
Andersen, the former Canadian turned Danish cycling guru, attributed the approach to nothing mag-
ical. "The Danes, the Dutch, the Germans, we're just
very practical. We just deal with it," he told me. This
attitude really struck home when I was chatting with

my expat Canadian hosts in Copenhagen. As she fought to light the wood-burning stove in her living room, which was set up across from her big flat-screen television, we spent a little time doing something very North American and bellyaching about how cold we were. She breathed a big sigh and said if felt good to moan about things that were out of her control. "Nobody here complains about anything," she said in frustration. She missed it.

That exchange said a lot to me about culturally different approaches to winter. For Canadians, and perhaps many North Americans, complaining about the weather has become second nature, our default way of relating to each other. While that's a nice way to connect with friends and strangers with a kind of instant bonding, and it gives us an outlet for our winter discontent, it also moulds our outlook on the season and, I think, helps explain our reluctance to embrace winter and, with it, winter cycling. For northern Europeans, their approach of unspoken acceptance has perhaps pushed their attitudes in a different direction, which helps explain why you see thousands of perfectly sane Danes riding bicycles through snowstorms.

While I was now several seasons into my mission to ride a bike all year round, when I noticed these differences I became convinced that I needed to change my own attitude toward winter to make the whole exercise less about battling the weather in the way that won Charley Gaul the Giro d'Italia. I needed my experience to be something more co-operative than confrontational. As I entered my third year of winter cycling, I decided to try to change my approach. No more would I suffer through winter and revel in the outsider status it gave me. My mission was to romp through it, and my sheer joy would change my own attitudes and convert those around me into winter believers.

Just how I was going to do that, however, I hadn't yet figured out.

CHAPTER 22

If I was to start to truly enjoy winter, I had to begin with what I had learned so far: those who have the most fun in winter seem to be those who are active in it. I was still riding my bike year-round, mostly to work, but I needed to do more. You can only derive so much pleasure from a commute – and I'm convinced the best way to derive any pleasure whatsoever is through cycling – but this went beyond commuting. Year-round cycling was still the goal, but to do that happily I needed to get beyond the grin-and-bear-it attitude that had taken me this far. Over the years, I had turned into a cycling proselytizer, but evangelists aren't great if they don't believe in their own cause. By trying to make winter more fun, I figured I would not only improve my winter cycling but also become a better winter cycling role model. I could prove to people around me that winter cycling really is a viable transportation option, and that maybe winter isn't so bad either. Perhaps that was expecting too much, but I needed some motivation, and this approach fit the bill.

So how does one go about changing a mindset related to something as fundamental as a season? That's where things got tricky. I didn't know where to start. So, inspired by a Christmas TV special my kids watched that year, in which Kris Kringle uses a jaunty song-and-dance number voiced by Mickey Rooney to encourage the Winter Warlock to start giving up his evil ways by "putting one foot in front of the other," I started small, with short forays outdoors after fresh snowfalls. I was lucky to have my kids around to do this with me. Having them frolic in the snow with me made the whole situation slightly less embarrassing when the neighbours watched me through their windows with eyebrows raised. The kids were great motivators to get outside, and they made it more enjoyable. Together we built snowmen and snow forts. I recalled my junior high outdoor education class teachings about building snow shelters called quinzhees (here's the basics: make a huge pile of snow; let it freeze a while; tunnel inside – toasty warm and fun, even when you bump your head on the ceiling and send snow down the back of your jacket). We invented new outdoor sports like snow soccer and mitten Frisbee.

We hauled our ice skates down to the neighbourhood outdoor rink, which reignited in me a dormant
love of pickup hockey. After 20 years of organized
games earlier in my life, I had forgotten the pure
pleasure of playing hockey outside with a bunch of
amateurs. Despite how it's sometimes portrayed, all
Canadians are not born with a love of hockey – in
fact, the number of kids playing the sport has been
slowly dwindling for years. This decline is often attributed to the high cost of the sport; the compet-
itive nature of minor hockey in Canada, which can
discourage newbies; and the changing demographics of the country, which is heavy on immigrants
from non-hockey-playing nations (even though
the popularity of watching the NHL is growing).
After a few Saturdays playing on the outdoor rink,
I now have a new theory about the decline in par-
ticipatory hockey: it's because fewer people are outside playing it informally. I had drifted away from
hockey since my childhood, but a few Saturday af-
ternoons of loosely organized shinny reminded me
why it's such a wonderful game.

It didn't take long to notice that all of these ef-
forts were starting to make an impact. I was actually
looking forward to time spent outdoors, so I took
the next step. Over the years, I had come to learn

that most of the people who claim to enjoy winter in my world were skiers and snowboarders. Living in a city along the foothills of the Rockies, within striking distance of some truly world-class ski resorts, skiing has long been a small part of life for many in the city, and an obsession for a minority. It was from those obsessed ones that I drew inspiration. I skied as a teenager, and became a regular snowboarder in my 20s, but when my kids were born, the snow gear went away. This isn't uncommon; a ski industry executive once told me that so many skiers give up when they have kids that new parents are specifically targeted by their marketing department. My kids were now old enough to try the sport, so my wife and I booked a weekend at a nearby ski resort, signed up the kids in day-long lessons, rented some gear and loaded up the minivan for a weekend away in late December (simply planning a holiday weekend in winter to a place that wasn't tropical seemed novel in itself).

I harboured some trepidation about hitting the slopes after so much time away. Things had changed. Skiing had undergone a revival, and had reclaimed some of the cachet that snowboarding had stolen in the 1990s. Some of this was due to changes in the equipment. The long planks I used when learning to ski had been replaced by shorter skis with curved edges that ski makers claimed were easier to use. They were right. While the kids were off on the bunny hill, my wife and I carved our way down the mountain like we were, well, riding a bike. In the crisp mountain air, surrounded by the splendour of snow-blanketed mountains, I found myself enjoying skiing more than I ever had before. I relished the scenery and the quiet times on the chair lift, and the energetic feeling my body had after a day of mountain exercise. The hot chocolates with Irish Cream I downed in the hot tub that evening certainly didn't hurt. Spending a weekend at a ski resort also provided a glimpse into the loveliness that a winter life can offer. I revelled in waking to a fresh snowfall every morning, especially knowing it would make the skiing better. Once we got over the fear of being buried by snow sliding off the slopeside village's steeply pitched rooftops, we began to appreciate the beauty of the cornices overlooking every rooftop. Being outside so often meant that braving the elements stopped being a chore – we even started clearing off a picnic table to eat lunch outdoors without much thought. Sure, comparing winter life at a ski resort to winter life at home is a bit like imagining you spend your summers at the Four Seasons Bora

Bora, but it gave me something to aspire to. My plan seemed to be working. Winter was fun. The more activities I took on, however, the more I realized something about the whole experience was bothering me. I couldn't quite put my finger on it, until I thought back to my time in Finland.

While I was there, I was most focused on learning about winter cycling in cities, but as I was out exploring, I remembered coming across groups of people out on the streets and pathways. Some were out jogging, wearing thermal running pants and thick mittens, but many were simply out walking. Large groups of senior citizens, all holding Nordic walking poles, were striding through the parks under fresh snowfalls. Of course, people go for constitutionals everywhere in the world, even in winter, but the scale in Finland was different. It seemed more a part of life for everyone to get outside in winter, even if it was just for a brisk walk. While riding beside the Oulu river one day with my new friend Pekka, near a dam that prevented the river from freezing over, we stopped so I could stare at a scene that was positively alien. Set up on the banks of the river was a portable trailer, with a metal gangway that stretched over the water. In the early morning darkness, I watched a fat, middle-aged Finn in a Speedo walk through the snow in bare feet and onto the metal dock. He used the attached ladder to lower himself into the freezing river, swam a few circles, and then climbed back out, his body steaming and his skin reddening in the cold. At home we call these "polar bear swims," and they are usually organized as mass novelty events during which suburban dads challenge each other to strip down and jump into the cold water for a few seconds to raise money for charity. But in Oulu, as Pekka pointed out, such cold-water swimming was so popular the city had installed an access point to the river and a change room. Pekka noticed my surprised look and said that some Finns think cold-water swimming is good for their health. "It's just what they like to do," he said with a shrug.

On its own, winter swimming may seem a little insane, but when combined with winter cycling, Nordic walking and winter jogging, it added up to a populace that managed to find a way to enjoy winter without making it an extreme sport as I was. Was this my problem? Was I unable to enjoy winter simply?

This thought encouraged me to dig out a book I had picked up in Finland called *Moomin in Winter*. Moomin is a comic-strip character that is part of the cultural fabric of Finland in the same way Mickey Mouse is in North America, except Moomin is a lumpy creature of uncertain origin with a massive nose. Everybody grows up on Moomin in Finland, so the stories, which tell the gentle misadventures of Moomin and his friends, are almost national folk tales. I had picked up the book to try to get a little insight into the character of Finns, but in the midst of my attempts to enjoy winter, I reread the story and realized something else. *Moomin in Winter* tells the tale of the Moomin family's attempts to hibernate for winter, until an insufferable jock comes by and bullies them into taking part in some outdoor winter sports. Things go awry for a while, until everyone learns to compromise, and the story ends with a nice winter party enjoyed by everyone. The story made me recognize that I had been acting a bit like that winter-sports tyrant. To think that living through winter requires sports or athletics was self-centred and naive. While it may have been working for me, it wasn't, as a Silicon Valley capitalist might say, scalable. Not everybody needed to enjoy winter the same way I did.

My next mission, therefore, became an uncomplicated, less aggressive attempt to make winter a bigger part of my life. I didn't quite muster up the nerve to start swimming in a half-frozen river, but I did start walking. For short errands or longer outings for pleasure, I eschewed the easy car hops of the past for simple, mindful rambles on foot.

Previously, walking in such conditions tended to be myopic experiences. I would pile on layers of clothing, wrap my head in a scarf leaving nothing exposed but my eyes while I charged forward with my head down and my mind on little but my destination. That doesn't make for pleasurable experiences, so I tried changing my style. I slowed my pace, lifted my eyes and looked for beauty in my surroundings. This can be a tall order. Winter in the city can be ugly. The sand and salt dumped on roads can become the dominant esthetic of the season, coating everything in a splattered brown slurry stubborn enough to stay until spring. Finding beauty in that can seem daunting.

Until, that is, you start to look with some purpose. Walking in the morning when everything is coated with hoarfrost is one of the more magical offerings of nature. Fresh snowfall can turn a brown and beaten city into a sparkling delight overnight. On some days, I took to stopping by the river to watch the water flow over and around buildups of ice, a beautiful and ever-changing jostling around the freezing point. Walking with my kids reminded me of the primal satisfaction of stomping through an ice buildup on a storm drain, or taking a run and sliding across a smooth patch of ice on a sidewalk. Ambling in this way revealed things that I had missed before. Even in an environment as urban as my neighbourhood, nature found a way to thrive. Snowbanks were peppered with the tracks of showshoe hares. In the river valleys, I saw coyotes digging for mice in the drifts beneath trees. I also noticed more people outdoors than I had realized before. The dog parks were filled with people and pets, and walking paths were bustling with joggers. These things had always been there, but I hadn't bothered to see them before. That obliviousness had been colouring my perception. Winter isn't as lonely and desolate as I once thought. Perhaps it can be whatever we want it to be. I was feeling better about winter, but I wasn't yet ready to declare victory. I had one other idea. Like Moomin, I would host a winter party as an attempt to embrace winter on terms that everybody could enjoy. I spelled out the plan to my wife: a backyard winter barbecue, with strings of lights, roaring campfires, hot chocolate and warm chili. It would be the kind of evening anyone could love, no matter the weather. She suspended her skepticism and helped me send invitations.

As the day neared, however, I started having

doubts. Who would want to give up a Saturday night to stand around in their galoshes in the cold? What if it snowed too much? What if the temperature dropped and we had to abandon the party just as it got going? The RSVPs, however, started coming back in droves. People liked the idea.

The day of the party wasn't exactly what I had envisioned. It was near the ides of March, still in the Canadian deep-freeze, but it hadn't snowed in weeks and the city was experiencing one of its periodic bouts of warm winter winds that left the yard brown and swampy, rather than snowy and twinkling like I had hoped. I dutifully plugged in the strings of lights and got the campfires roaring while my wife brewed vats of hot chocolate and set out bottles of schnapps to add a little more warmth, and people came. Wearing novelty party hats with wool liners, and towing excited children bouncing on boots with LED lights built into the heels, they ate chili dogs and drank us out of hot chocolate. We caught up with neighbours we hadn't spoken to since the last round of lawn mowing six months before. We cracked jokes, gossiped and laughed. After a while, the event ceased being a winter party and became just a party. We no longer cared what season it was, or what the temperature was, or what we had to wear to keep warm. We just enjoyed ourselves.

Eventually, I began to lighten up about the outdoor conditions. Sure, it may not have been the winter wonderland I had in mind when I planned it, but nobody seemed to care. As the partygoers left and we began to clean up, my mind wasn't on the season, or my ongoing battle with my own attitude toward winter. I was thinking about the party and the friends who enjoyed it with us. The weather had become an afterthought. It felt good. For one evening, we didn't battle winter, and we didn't avoid it. We coexisted. Rather than succumbing to the season, we had reached an understanding. Mother Nature will never lose her infinite indifference to us, but I felt, for that night at least, we finally accepted something we had always fought against. Perhaps it was the schnapps making itself comfortable in my body, but that thought gave me some peace. Despite the brown lawn and the soupy mess created by the campfire thawing the frozen topsoil, I felt a little more at home that night.

Did the party change anybody's attitude toward winter? That's difficult to say. I'm sure some partygoers grumbled about their muddy boots the next morning. All I know is that I felt a change.

I awoke to a fresh snowfall that had beautified everything with the sparkle and muffled sounds that I had grown to love. The snow was still falling in big, lazy flakes that softened the world and swathed everything in a comforting layer of white. I dressed warmly and wheeled my bike out of the garage. Beneath dull sunlight filtered by the falling snow, I pushed off into an untouched blanket of velvety powder and pedalled my way through the city.

EPILOGUE

A year after the winter party, a group of cycling advocates in my city launched a do-it-yourself mid-winter bicycle festival that included nighttime pleasure rides, a bike-to-work day that offered free coffee and doughnuts to commuters, and even a night of bike racing on ice using studded tires. It wasn't the first festival in the world to promote the idea of year-round riding by trying to make it fun and inclusive. Rather, it was an idea that had been spreading across the winter world for several years, and had finally come to my city. Considering that winter cycling was once perceived as a pastime for zealots and masochists, I took the festival as a sign that things were changing.

As I was writing this book, something else happened. Through my blog, I received a message from a professor of civil engineering at the University of Calgary named Dr. Farnaz Sadeghpour. As part of her attempts to teach engineering undergrads the importance of engaging with the public on civic issues, she had her students head outdoors in the depths of winter to survey winter cyclists. They stopped thousands of people on bikes and asked questions about their winter cycling habits. Her students had collected several years of data and, she wondered, was I interested in seeing it?

One evening, I trudged up to her campus office and she gave me a peek at the data she had been collecting. My jaw dropped. Her students asked cyclists a barrage of questions, from the frequency and purpose of their winter cycling trips to the distance they most often travelled to the coldest temperatures in which they were willing to ride a bike. Data like this existed almost nowhere in the world, yet here, in my own city, Dr. Sadeghpour had quietly been building a treasure trove of information. What it revealed was fascinating, and both confirmed and contradicted some long-held assumptions about winter cyclists.

What struck me first was the demographic information. In most cities, cyclists tend to be athletic young men who are confident and even aggressive riders. This doesn't bode well for the mainstream acceptance of cycling, so advocates are always looking at ways of encouraging cycling among women, the young, the old and the timid. I had assumed winter would exacerbate that demographic problem. What Dr. Sadeghpour's surveys revealed, however, was that most winter cyclists were men over the age of 44, which told me that perhaps winter cycling wasn't the extreme sport that most people assumed. Other survey questions revealed that most winter cyclists consider snow and ice as their biggest concern, even more so than the presence and quality of dedicated bike infrastructure. Most also said they own a car, which meant they chose to ride rather than drive in winter, and most were on trips longer than 10 kilometres, which is a huge distance compared to surveys from other cities, all of which were taken in the summer.

The most enlightening piece of data revealed by Dr. Sadeghpour's surveys, however, related to temperature. I had always assumed that my limit for winter cycling of about -20°C (-4°F) would be about as cold as most people would be willing to endure, and I always viewed my willingness to brave that frigid temperature as an anomaly. It turns out that I'm not very special. More than half of people surveyed said they would ride to -20°C (-4°F) or even colder. A big chunk of respondents said they would ride no matter how cold it got. Considering many arguments against cycling in northern cities circle around an assumption that it's too cold to ride for much of the year, this data is illuminating. Assuming we can apply the findings to other cities (scientifically, of course, we cannot, because answers may differ from place to place, but I'd bet survey respondents would answer similarly elsewhere), consider the civic climate data presented earlier. If more than half of winter cyclists are willing to brave -20°C (-4°F) or colder, that means there are very few days in which it would be considered too cold to ride: in most winter cities in North America, such as Minneapolis, Montreal and my city of Calgary, that's about 20 days a year. This may be a game-changing piece of data. If there are only 20 days a year too cold for most winter cyclists, it suddenly becomes very difficult to argue against building bike infrastructure based on the assumption that it will go unused for much of the year.

There are still many unanswered questions about winter cycling. Dr. Sadeghpour hopes to use her survey to conduct a more accurate count of winter cyclists in the future, for example. This kind of work also needs to be done in other winter cities. In thinking about winter cycling, however, I took both the existence of her survey, and the findings it revealed, as a sign that the idea isn't as absurd as it is sometimes portrayed. Still, the question that had started me on my journey and drove this book still lingered in my mind. Could winter cycling be a viable and pleasurable way of getting around?

In some ways, the question had become answerable with a resounding yes. The popularity of fat-biking as a recreational sport, for example, continues to grow. Those massive tires have spawned a new winter sport that is growing in popularity more quickly than anybody anticipated. Off-road trails in many areas of North America are being opened up for fat bikers to enjoy. Ski resorts are turning areas over to them. Winter races are cropping up all over the place. A sign of the sport's popularity are the conflicts that have begun to emerge. Fat bikers and cross-country skiers have started to argue over trail use in some areas, in the same ways that hikers and mountain bikers once argued about summertime mountain trails. These conflicts will no doubt work themselves out, and forward-looking planners are already recognizing the recreational and tourism opportunities that fat bikes can afford. I'm even starting to see more fat bikes being used as commuting vehicles.

In other ways, however, the question about winter cycling isn't so simple to answer. On a personal level, it's a no-brainer. I'm motivated to ride because I enjoy it, it's great exercise, it gets me around quickly, and every once in a while I find myself in the midst of one of those majestic winter moments that acts as a lingering motivator. Cities will always have dedicated year-round cyclists – an increasing number of them by the looks of it – who feel the same way. Urban cycling, however, is no longer just a personal thing. It has ramifications far beyond individual riders, and as the benefits of increasing the number of people on bikes become impossible to ignore, cycling is also becoming increasingly political. Bike infrastructure often sparks a vociferous backlash from some automobile drivers, even when it's been proven repeatedly that well-planned bike lanes make transportation systems more efficient and safe for everyone. Winter adds a new element to that reaction, and understandably so. Compared to the number of bicycle commuters in summer, winter numbers remain small in most jurisdictions. So it's reasonable to ask if it's worth investing taxpayer money on bike infrastructure in cold cities.

My time riding through winter has given me some perspective on that question. If we want our urbanites to enjoy the true benefits of cycling, we need more than just the confident and committed. As Copenhagen's Mikael Colville-Andersen says, we don't need more "cyclists" on the road, we need more people on bikes. He means we don't need more athletic dudes dressed in Lycra bombing around as a form of exercise. Instead, we need more regular people choosing the bike as a simple, fast and efficient form of getting around the city. What's stopping them? If polls are to be believed – and I've seen surveys from half a dozen North American cities with similar results – a majority of people say they would like to ride their bicycles more but don't feel safe. So we need to remove risk and make it easier for everybody to ride. That often means building bike routes that are secure, calm and direct, which in many cases will mean separated from motorized vehicles. When women, children and the elderly, not just aggressive young men, start to see the bike as an easy way to go shopping, to school or to work, then our cities will start to enjoy improvements in our street life, our economy, our health and our transportation systems.

With that in mind, winter is not a reason to neglect measures to make life easier for cyclists. Dedicated bike lanes are even more important in winter than summer because the risk of slipping into the path of a vehicle is greater on snow and ice. In colder weather, cyclists also need short and efficient routes to their destinations. Winter maintenance, such as snow removal, plowing and ice control are vital. This infrastructure is most important in denser urban areas because that's where distances to workplaces tend to be short enough to make cycling most viable. We shouldn't, however, forget the suburbs. There are plenty of people who would bike long distances in winter if it was made easier.

Will we ever get enough winter cyclists to justify the costs of building segregated bike lanes? That is a specious question. The number of cyclists will always fall when it gets colder, but winter cycling doesn't exist on its own. It's part of a year-round movement. Bike infrastructure can work wonders for most of the year, and having it used less frequently for a few winter months doesn't negate its need. City planners unquestioningly invest in all kinds of things that are largely seasonal, from baseball diamonds to playgrounds to snow plows. All of these make our cities more livable even if they lie dormant for a season. Bike infrastructure can make lives better year-round.

The longer I've thought about the question of winter cycling, the more I have come to realize the importance of our attitudes. Our personal and collective outlooks on winter are key to the mass acceptance of year-round cycling. Yet attitude doesn't exist in a vacuum. It is informed by the world we live in. In the case of winter cycling, it is heavily swayed by practical considerations. The type of bike we choose, the routes we travel on, and the conditions in which we ride are important. Feelings of comfort and safety have a heavy influence on the way we perceive cycling. If those winter experiences are positive, they can change our outlook. There is a societal role in this. A city that encourages year-round cycling also helps normalize it. That's how perceptions change.

There is also a big personal role in making winter cycling viable. When I started working on this book, I revelled in the identity that winter cycling gave me. I liked being perceived as the tough and resilient commuter who could handle the depths of the season. The more I explored, however, the more I found that image being challenged. As I got better at finding the pleasures of winter, I realized that doing so was not as difficult as I once thought. The practical and the psychological seemed to build upon each other to change my point of view. I see now the enjoyment of winter needn't be an aberration. In fact, it's not. If you are looking, you'll see innumerable people revelling in the season in innumerable ways. Whereas once I enjoyed being seen as an outsider, now I know it's a needless, myopic myth. We can all be winter cyclists.

I'm not saying winter is easy. It's not. After four or five months of cold, April snowstorms exasperate me as much as anybody. I have learned, however, that I have more control over winter's influence on me than I once thought. Technology has given us the ability to mitigate the impact of the season on our lives like never before. Rather than using that technology to remove winter from my life as much as possible, I'm going to work on removing only the hard parts. I want to make the season easier and more enjoyable without eliminating it completely. This approach, I think, is just as important to the viability of winter cycling as finding the right bike and building the right infrastructure, and they all work together.

Is winter cycling viable? It already is, at least in a small way. It is making us healthier and more engaged in our cities and our own lives. It is making our cities friendlier, less hostile, cleaner, healthier and more fun. It is helping us work toward a cleaner climate, at a time when that has never been more important. It is even changing how we think about winter, making it seem less otherworldly and hostile. So perhaps asking about viability is the wrong question. Maybe we should ask what's holding more of us back? The answer is simple: we are.

Fortunately, that's the easiest thing to change. Can we convert entire cities of car drivers into year-round cyclists? Probably not, at least in the short term, and that shouldn't be the goal. In fact, maybe we shouldn't try to change anybody at all. We just need to work on ourselves.

Recently, I was riding my bike to work during a typical morning commute. It was cold, so I had to talk myself into cycling that day, but within a few minutes of pedalling, as is always the case, I was glad I did. My internal engine started humming and warming my body, and my mood improved. I breezed past a group of people waiting for the bus, most of them underdressed for the cold weather and shivering. As I picked up my pace, I overtook a driver in a huge SUV, coffee in one hand, the other on the steering wheel, barking into her hands-free cellphone, the end of her scarf hanging out the bottom of the door and getting sprayed with mud. At a four-way stop, a blue-collar worker in a big pickup truck helpfully waved me through the intersection. I happily pedalled on.

As I neared my office, I came to a paved pathway that I look forward to on days of snow because I get to lay fresh tracks. This time, however, somebody had beaten me to it. I didn't think much of it, until I pulled into the front of the office and saw another bike in the rack. I locked my ride and headed up the stairs. On my way, I ran into a co-worker who seemed excited to see me.

"Hey, guess what I did today," he said. "I rode my bike to work."

TIPS FOR WINTER CYCLING

Since I first started cycling in winter, some of the most consistent questions I have encountered were the practical ones: how do you do it?

My answers have varied over the years, but I have come to a few conclusions, and while they may still be subject to change, hopefully they add up to some practical tips for anybody interested in winter cycling. They may not turn you into a die-hard lover of winter, but this advice has worked for me and I feel comfortable passing it along.

There is, however, a caveat to go along with what I suggest, which may sound like a cop-out but I mean it sincerely. The best advice I can give on how to ride a bike year-round is this: figure it out for yourself. There is much variance in climate, cities and cyclists, so strategies that work for one person may be totally meaningless to another. I live in a climate prone to freeze–melt cycles, for example, so one of my major concerns is ice. That means studded tires work wonders. If you live in a climate with consistent winter temperatures below the freezing point, however, you may rarely encounter slippery spots, so studded tires may be needless. That said, here's what may be applicable elsewhere:

The bike

Use fenders.

Use lights. For many people, the shorter, darker days are the most difficult part of winter cycling. Reflectors alone don't cut it. LED bike lights these days are cheap and ultra-efficient. Buy some for the front and back of your bike, and maybe your head – headlamps work well.

Use studded tires. Winter tires are a must for your car, so why not your bike?

People in North American don't like to hear this because we tend to like having specialized gear for every job, but you don't need a special bike to ride in winter. Use any bike you want, but wash it regularly. If your garden hose is frozen or shut off in winter, take your bike to a car wash every once in a while. A dollar's worth of spray will work wonders. If there's no car wash nearby, fill up a bucket in the kitchen sink and scrub your bike down every week or two.

If you are determined to have a second bike for winter, you don't need to spend too much money on it. In the slushy climate I live in, in which sand, salt, grit and meltwater come together like a corrosive smoothie, I've ruined a handful of bikes through rust. To prevent that, I've learned to avoid riding any bike that I care about in the winter. My current winter machine is a 20-year-old aluminum-framed mountain bike that I picked up at a used bike shop for $50. I stripped off the gears, the front and back derailleurs and anything else that might collect junk, and turned the bike into a single speed using a $10 conversion kit. It's not perfect – one gear can be tough riding on hills – but it's worked for me.

If you hate cleaning your bike, buy an old used mountain bike, ride it until the components are dead, then strip them and start over with new parts. If that costs too much, go to a wealthy area of your city and troll the back alleys a day or two before garbage pickup. You're bound to come across a discarded bike that you can get working after a little maintenance. If the rich area of town doesn't work, go to the poorest. The neighbourhoods in the middle tend not to work. Look for an aluminum frame, because it's lighter and won't rust, and don't get too attached to it, because your lazy cleaning schedule may end up killing it.

If, however, you are the type of cyclist who needs top-end gear, I understand. We're all gearheads at heart. Read on.

If you want to ride a top-end bike for recreation, go for a fat bike. The extra-large tires are fun to ride, and will keep you entertained all winter. They work on road or off, and adjust to all kinds of conditions, from moderately deep snow to slush. Fat bikes open up a whole new season of possibilities. These bikes also work for commuting, but may be too slow and expensive for your needs.

If your primary goal is urban riding or commuting, consider buying a European-style all-season bike if you can afford it. There are many models that include internal gears to keep out the elements, disc brakes and lights powered by hub dynamos that generate electricity from the turning of the wheel. In the right climate, this kind of bike can provide years of safe, predictable, all-season riding.

If you can't afford that, or feel like a dandy riding it, there are a couple of things you can do. First, get over yourself. You look fine. But if price is a problem, consider a single-speed or fixed-gear bike. They have fewer parts to collect snow, moisture and, consequently, rust. Fixies offer more control than single-speeds but don't allow you to coast down the hills, and they take some practice to ride.

If your commute is too long or hilly for a single-speed or fixed-gear – my ride to work is about 15 kilometres, and I'd say that's about the farthest you'd want to go on such a bike – look for a bike with the fewest gears that will get to your destination. I'm of the opinion that most commuter bikes these days are loaded with three or four times more gears than you actually need. Most bikes I found in Europe had three or six gears, and that was more than enough to get around a city.

If you have one of those epically long commutes that North American newspaper reporters like to write about as if they are novelties for the deranged, thereby making bike commuting seem like something reserved for extreme athletes and the extremely insane (yes, I've written those stories), I have two additional pieces of advice:

1. Don't talk to reporters.
2. Pay a bike shop to build a bike like this: cyclo-cross frame, which is as light and fast as a road bike but features more clearance in the forks for wider tires; the widest tires you can fit, studded; disc brakes; full gearing enclosed in a chain guard; fenders; and a rack that will carry panniers. This won't be cheap, but it could also serve as your summer bike simply by removing the studded tires.

My last piece of advice on the bike you use for winter riding is to reiterate my first: most of these suggestions are needless. You don't need a special bike. Just ride. Consider it an experiment and adjust as you go.

The clothing

The Internet is full of advice on what to wear when cycling in the winter. Most of it is useless. Here is all you need to know: dress warm and dry. Whatever you wear to keep warm while walking, skiing or sledding in winter will work just fine. The only special equipment you might need will be one of those bands that wraps around your ankle to keep your pants away from the bike chain, although a five-cent elastic band works just as well.

Wear one layer less than you'd wear if going for a walk. You'll warm up as your body starts to move. In fact, you should be a little cold when you start your ride. If you start out too warm, you'll end up arriving at your destination looking like you just emerged from a sauna. It's easy to underestimate the heat-generating powers of your body.

If you are commuting to work and arrive too sweaty, try wearing fewer clothes, but finding the sweet spot between too cold and too warm can be tough. Another option is to slow down. It's not a race. If you find this impossible, consider using a different commuter bike. Speedy bikes make you want to go fast. If you want to go slow, try a slower bike. You likely won't take significantly more time to get to work, and you'll save time because you won't need a shower when you arrive.

If you want to get a good workout by cycling in the winter, or are riding for recreation, make sure you dress in layers. Lobster gloves, or three-finger gloves, work well because they keep your fingers warm while giving your fingers the dexterity to shift gears. Mittens keep your hands warmest, but be sure you can still reach the shifters. You can also try pogies, which are oversized mittens that attach to handlebars over the shifters and brakes. You reach inside them to ride, and they do a great job keeping hands warm while still enabling you to work the brakes and shifters. A thin headwarmer, such as a balaclava, wool hat or toque, beneath your helmet if you wear one, is usually enough to keep warm once your body starts moving. Pay particular attention to keeping your feet warm by wearing decent boots and wool socks. Don't overdress – excessive sweating in the winter is bad because you will freeze when your body finally stops moving.

Keeping dry is also important. The best thing you can do to keep water off your body is to install fenders on your bike. If it's an especially wet day, you may also find the need to wear a thin, waterproof outer layer, but such clothing tends to be hot and will make you sweat, which will defeat the entire purpose of trying to stay dry. The solution to this problem is to slow down.

The city

There are many things cities can do to make cycling easier and more efficient in winter, so if you are a politician, a city bureaucrat, a bike advocate, a citizen, or a human with transportation needs, here's what I've seen that works.

If your city is not bike friendly, don't worry too much about winter cycling. Just get some bike infrastructure built. The benefits of dedicated bike lanes have been proven again and again, and they are true in all seasons. Advocate, campaign, organize and celebrate victories. Don't wait for a huge number of cyclists before building, because they will never come; the reason the majority of people don't ride is because of a lack of safe infrastructure. In most cities, installing safe and efficient bike lanes has led to big growth in the numbers of people on bikes.

Bike infrastructure opponents often trot out winter as a reason a city might be unfit for cycling. This is false. Every city has its unique climatic challenges, hot, cold or windy, but we've yet to see any city that doesn't benefit from bike infrastructure. Remember that three of the most bike-friendly cities in North America also have serious winters: Montreal, Minneapolis and Anchorage. If they can do it, so can your city.

Try not to mention European cycling cities like Amsterdam or Copenhagen in these discussions, because that makes bike infrastructure seem exotic and foreign. Also, avoid dipping into the climate-change argument in support of cycling. Yes, bikes are good for the environment, but the argument is a nonstarter in North America. Very few people ride a bike for environmental reasons. They do it because it's fun, fast and efficient and makes their community, their city and their life better.

Don't fall for hare-brained ideas like summer-only bike lanes. Winter doesn't negate the need for bike-friendly infrastructure, it exacerbates it. If a separated bike lane makes people feel safe in the summer, it will be needed even more in the winter.

Don't be discouraged by smaller cyclist numbers in the winter. It's natural that fewer people bike year-round. That doesn't remove the need for bike infrastructure. Fewer people also go for walks and drive cars in the winter; that doesn't mean we should stop building roads or clearing snow from the sidewalks. Plus, municipalities are already packed with seasonal stuff, from parks to snow plows to street cleaners, so it's not unusual to build infrastructure more heavily used in summer. Snow and ice make many people wary of riding a bike, so the need for infrastructure is greater in the winter.

Plow. Plow early and often. Clear snow from bike lanes before roads. If your city is going to build a bike lane, make sure they have a plow that will fit (this is a problem more common than you might think).

Sand and salt when necessary. Plows don't always do the trick. With so many different kinds of winter weather, your city may need to adopt different kinds of winter maintenance to keep bike lanes safe. We do this for roads, so we should do it for bike lanes too. Yes, salt damages the environment and rusts bikes, but it's the best option in some conditions.

Maintain bike infrastructure based on conditions, not precipitation. Most cities send out plows only after it snows, but freezing meltwater, condensation, and ice buildup can all happen between snowfalls.

The best tactic is to monitor conditions constantly, and treat them accordingly.

Make sure there's a place to keep the snow after it's removed from the bike lane. Poorly planned lanes can create situations in which snow is plowed from a bike lane into a car lane, and then back again. Make sure infrastructure is built with space to store snow. Windrows of snow can make a nice separation between car and bike lanes, and cyclists feel safer, provided there is still enough room for a bike.

Bike lanes painted on roads don't work very well in winter. For one thing, snow covers them up and makes them invisible. Secondly, snow tends to get thrown from cars into the bike lane, creating slippery, dangerous conditions. Ideally, there should be a barrier between the two, or at least enough space to prevent spillover.

Fat-biking holds the potential to be a huge new winter recreational opportunity. If your city has mountain bike trails that close in the winter, convince officials to keep them open year round. If your municipality has cross-country ski trails, make space for fat bikes. If you operate a ski hill, carve out a place for fat-biking.

Your attitude

If the biggest hurdle to winter cycling is ourselves, that's also the easiest thing to fix. Here's a little advice on getting over yourself and your fears.

Just try it. If you've been mulling over a winter bike commute or recreational ride, but are wary about it, just go for it. If it doesn't work, so be it. If it does, congratulations: your life will be better.

Approach winter cycling with an attitude of experimentation. If something isn't working, change it. Years later, I'm still constantly adjusting things. Part of the fun is finding things that work.

Forget your machismo. One of the biggest obstacles facing urban winter bike commuting is the perception that it's only for crazy masochists. This isn't the case. Riding a bike in winter doesn't need to be tough. It is not an extreme sport, so don't act like it is. Resist the urge to brag.

Don't be a zealot. If you can only manage to bicycle commute one winter day a week, or only hit recreational trails when the weather is mild, don't think of yourself as a failure. You are not competing against anyone or anything. If you're in the midst of a cold snap, take the bus. Just make inroads where you can. Every little bit you can do will make you a happier, healthier person.

Get realistic about the weather. In nearly every city I've looked at, people tend to exaggerate their winter. Most cities have many more mild winter days than extremely cold ones. Remember, when looking at a weather forecast, the predicted low temperature usually happens in the middle of the night when you are fast asleep in your warm bed. You'll be riding in warmer temperatures than that and you'll probably surprise yourself by how warm you'll be once your body gets moving. My biggest winter biking challenge isn't staying warm; it's staying cool enough that I don't sweat.

Don't fear the snow. Snow is usually only a problem if it's several feet deep and hasn't been plowed. If you do slip and crash into this kind of snow, you're more likely to laugh than injure yourself. Remember, snow can be fun. It can be a lovely experience to ride through a snowfall. I'm convinced laying fresh tracks is a primal human instinct because it feels so good. Fear the ice, but be realistic about it. Ice is a danger, but in most places it is easily avoided. Stay alert and ride around icy patches. If you must cross over ice, stay straight and upright and don't touch your brakes. If there is a lot of ice on your ride, studded tires are an easy, relatively affordable solution. They work. Use them. Be wary of road snirt. Snirt is a mixture of snow and dirt (hence, snirt) pounded by passing cars into a brown mixture with the consistency of mashed potatoes. While it may appear harmless, it can be deadly. It tends to float on top of packed snow, and will move your bike in sudden, unpredictable ways that never end well. Even studded tires are no match for some snirt. Avoid it at all costs.

Get outside. If you still think riding in the winter is a loony idea, try to get outdoors in the winter a little more. Go for a walk or a jog. Go skiing. Go ice-skating. Play pond hockey. Sled down a hill. As long as you dress accordingly, you might be surprised at how manageable winter is and how much fun you were missing out on.

REFERENCES

"America's Top 50 Bike-Friendly Cities." *Bicycling Magazine*, accessed 15 Feb. 2014. http://www.bicycling.com/news/advocacy/america's-top-50-bike-friendly-cities.

Analitis, A., K. Katsouyanni, A. Biggeri, M. Baccini, B. Forsberg, L. Bisanti, U. Kirchmayer, F. Ballester, E. Cadum, P.G. Goodman, A. Hojs, J. Sunyer, P. Tiittanen, and P. Michelozzi. "Effects of Cold Weather on Mortality: Results From 15 European Cities Within the PHEWE Project." *American Journal of Epidemiology* 168.12 (2008): 1397–1408, full accessed 3 Aug. 2013. http://aje.oxfordjournals.org/content/168/12/1397.

Berton, Pierre. *Winter.* Toronto: Stoddart, 1994.

"Best Inventions of 2003: Transportation: Ice Bike" *Time Magazine* (Dec. 2003), accessed 5 Aug. 2013. http://content.time.com/time/specials/packages/article/0,28804,1935038_1935083_1935722,00.html.

"Bicycling Enthusiasts Pack Madison Square Garden." *New York Times* (21 Jan. 1896): n.p.

"Climate at a Glance." National Climatic Data Center (NCDC). National Oceanic and Atmospheric Association, accessed 15 Feb. 2014. http://www.ncdc.noaa.gov/cag/.

Cole, Terrence, ed. *Wheels on Ice: Bicycling in Alaska 1898–1908.* Northern History Library. Anchorage, AL: Alaska Northwest Publishing Company, 1985.

Coleman, Patrick. "Winter Community." *The Review: The Official Magazine of the Michigan Municipal League.* (January, February 2010), accessed 27 May 2013. http://www.mml.org/resources/publications/mmr/pdf/jan-feb2010mag.pdf.

Colville-Andersen, Mikael. "Green Light Go – The Birth of Cycle Chic." Flickr. Yahoo! (07 Aug. 2008), accessed 27 May 2013. https://www.flickr.com/photos/16nine/sets/72157594400316816.

"Copenhagenize.com – Bicycle Culture by Design," accessed 20 May 2013. http://www.copenhagenize.com.

"Copenhagenize.eu" *The Copenhagenize Index of Bicycle Friendly Cities,* accessed 2 May 2013. http://www.copenhagenize.com/2013/04/copenhagenize-index-2013-bicycle.html.

DeMarban, Alex. "Alaska's Fat-bike Mania Spreads Its Tire Track across World." *Alaska Dispatch* (27 Dec. 2011), accessed 5 Aug. 2013. http://www.alaskadispatch.com/article/alaskas-fat-bike-mania-spreads-its-tire-track-across-world-0.

Donaldson, G.C., V.E. Tchernjavskii, S.P. Ermakov, K. Bucher, and W.R. Keatinge. "Winter Mortality and Cold Stress in Yekaterinburg, Russia: Interview Survey."

BMJ (1998): 316–514, accessed 3 Aug. 2013. http://dx.doi.
org/10.1136/bmj.316.7130.514.

Eirtou, Anthony. "Four-going the Conventional." *Winning*
(1990): 64, accessed 3 Mar. 2014. http://forums.mtbr.
com/fat-bikes/steve-baker-icicle-bicycles-855673.html.

Embacher, Michael. *Cyclepedia: A Century of Iconic
Bicycle Design*. Photographs by Bernhard Angerer. San
Francisco: Chronicle Books, 2011.

Environment Canada. "Canadian Climate Normals."
Environment Canada, accessed 15 Feb. 2014. http://cli-
mate.weather.gc.ca/climate_normals/.

Fotheringham, William. "Charly Gaul." *The Guardian* (8
Dec. 2005), accessed 15 Feb. 2014. http://www.theguard-
ian.com/news/2005/dec/08/guardianobituaries.cycling.

"Gold Strike Near Dawson; A Report that Fort Yukon
Has Been Burned Not Verified – Plenty to Eat in
the Klondike." *New York Times*, 14 Nov. 1897, accessed
March 3, 2014. http://query.nytimes.com/mem/ar-
chive-free/pdf?res=F30915F9385416738DDDAD0994
D9415B8785F0D3.

Gopnik, Adam. *Winter: Five Windows on the Season*.
Toronto: Anansi, 2011.

Guy, William A., M.B. "On the Annual Fluctuations in
the Number of Deaths from Various Diseases, compared with like Fluctuations in Crime and in other
Events within and beyond the Control of the Human
Will." *Journal of the Statistical Society of London* 21 (Mar.

1858): 52–86, accessed 27 May 2013. https://archive.org/stream/jstor-2338211/2338211#page/n1/mode/2up.

Kahney, Leander. "Alaskan Snow Bike Rolls into Sunny California." *Wired Magazine*, Conde Nast Digital (18 Apr. 2009), accessed 5 Aug. 2013. http://www.wired.com/gadgetlab/2009/04/alaskan-snow-bi.

"Kottke National End of Season Survey 2011/2012." National Ski Areas Association, accessed 26 July 2013. http://www.nsaa.org/.

Medred, Craig. "Alaskan's Creations Conquer Snow, but Face Cost Challenges from Outside." *Anchorage Daily News* (26 Nov. 2006): n.p.

"Montreal's Winter Carnival." *The New York Times* (23 Feb. 1884): n.p.

"Montreal's Winter Carnival." *The New York Times* (23 Jan. 1887): n.p.

Moodie, Susanna. *Roughing It in the Bush; Or, Life in Canada*. London: R. Bentley, 1852.

National Operational Hydrologic Remote Sensing Center. "Snow Data Assimilation System (SNODAS) data products at NSIDC." Boulder, CO: National Snow and Ice Data Center, 2004. Digital media.

Niziol, Tom. "Why The Weather Channel Is Naming Winter Storms." The Weather Channel (11 Nov. 2012), accessed 26 July 2013. http://www.weather.com/news/why-we-name-winter-storms-20121001.